Coming Home

Coming Home

Life, Love, and All Things Southern

Robert Inman

Down Home Press, Asheboro, N.C.

ISBN 1-878086-86-3

Library of Congress control number 00-133351

Printed in the United States of America

Book design by Beth Hennington

Jacket design by Tim Rickard

Down Home Press
P.O. Box 4126
Asheboro, N.C. 27204

Distributed by John F. Blair, Publisher, 1406 Plaza Dr., Winston-Salem, N.C. 27103

for
Lee Bancroft Inman

Introduction

"Just say I'm a small-town kid and a storyteller," I tell anyone who's going to introduce me to an audience. "That just about sums me up."

If they read my printed resume, folks think I'm a fellow who never could hold down a regular job. At various times I have mowed lawns, sold hardware, toted a rifle, taught school, been a public relations mouthpiece for a politician and a college, raised young'uns, delivered newspapers, had speaking parts on radio and television, and scribbled things on paper. A few years ago I left my longest-running job, one of those TV speaking parts, to scribble full-time. I think it's what I want to do when I grow up.

I'm first of all a small-town kid. A Southern small-town kid. My hometown marked me with permanent ink and in ways I discover daily. A small town is a small stage upon which life's comedy and drama play out in full view of everyone, and if you're curious and observant enough, you can learn a lot about people and what makes them tick. In my hometown, there is one of just about every kind of character you can imagine. They are people who are worth telling stories about, and since I grew up in a family of storytellers, I suppose it's just natural that I do what I do.

Then too, I come from a long line of folks

who are determined to have their say. I trace my lineage to the Coopers who helped settle Sampson County, North Carolina in the 1700's. Several were Baptist preachers. One of them, Fleet Cooper, was a signer of the Mecklenburg Declaration of Independence, which some historians claim preceded the better-known document by a couple of years. One relative was killed at the Battle of Kings Mountain, and several others fought the British near Wilmington. They must have been a stubborn and sometimes ornery lot, given to stirring up things and speaking their minds. I fit right in.

Herein you will find some of my stories, many of them about small-town folks, and some assorted thoughts, large and small, that have occurred to me over the years. I've been around long enough to have participated in some foolishness and tasted some of the tart and the sweet of life. My family and friends have put up with a lot. I reward them by writing about them, though many times they'd just as soon I didn't.

A special note of thanks to Jennie Buckner, Ed Williams and Jane Pope of the *Charlotte Observer,* who let me do some of my scribbling in their Sunday paper. They let me write about most anything that occurs to me, and so far I haven't gotten them sued. A fair deal on both sides, don't you think?

Contents

III. *Life with Father*

IV. *My Friend Delbert Earle*

V. He Stares Out the Window a Lot

A Small-town Kid and a Storyteller

Mama Cooper and the Tax Man

Whenever April 15th rolls around, I think about my grandmother. Nell Bancroft Cooper was an upright, law-abiding citizen. Except for once. And it had to do with the tax man.

Mama Cooper lived most of her life in a two-story white frame house on Buford Street in Elba, Alabama. When I was a small boy, there were two equally-gracious older homes across the street from Mama Cooper.

At the time, Elba's housewives did their grocery shopping at two small mom-and-pop stores on the courthouse square several blocks away. The selection was limited and the walk downtown, especially on a blistering summer day, could be a chore.

Then, in the mid-'50s, came the Piggly Wiggly. The supermarket chain announced that it would build a gleaming modern store in Elba. Folks got excited about what they considered a hallmark of economic and cultural progress. That is, until Piggly Wiggly announced its location; right across Buford Street from Mama Cooper's house. The Piggly Wiggly folks bought those two gracious old homes, bulldozed them, and built the supermarket. Most folks in Elba viewed the matter with ambivalent alarm. Progress, yes. But demolishing two pieces of the town's history?

Mama Cooper had no qualms at all. Ever the pragmatist, she viewed the Piggly Wiggly as convenience, pure and simple. It was marvelous to be able to walk a hundred yards from your front door into the air-conditioned comfort of a well-stocked supermarket. There would be no hot treks to the courthouse square, and she could buy what she needed when she needed it, a decided advantage due to the capacity of the tiny, antique refrigerator in her kitchen. Other town folks, she said in so many words, should get a grip.

Piggly Wiggly, aware no doubt of the controversy surrounding the new Elba store, announced that the opening would be accompanied by a prize give-away. Whenever you made a purchase, you would receive a prize card. If you could match the numbers on two cards, you would win a prize — ranging from a small grocery item to a $1,000 grand prize.

One warm June morning shortly after the store opened, Mama Cooper checked her pantry and discovered that she was out of peanut butter. So she put on her hat, picked up her purse, and marched smartly to the Piggly Wiggly where she purchased one small jar of peanut butter. She got a prize card.

Late that same afternoon, Mama Cooper decided on her supper menu — a glass of buttermilk and a peanut butter and banana sandwich. She found that she was out of bananas so she armed herself with hat and purse and returned to the Piggly Wiggly. She got another prize card. She compared it with the one she had received that morning, still in her purse, and calmly announced, "I've just won the grand prize."

You can imagine the commotion. Townsfolk were delighted and envious over what Elba, in the mid-'50s, considered a huge windfall. And the *way* she had won it evoked the kind of awe and wonder previously reserved for the Great Flood of '29.

Everybody asked Mama Cooper what she planned to do with the money. Members of her immediate family were especially interested. Every one of us had a great idea for helping her spend it. But to one and all, she was maddeningly non-committal. In fact, she went to the grave years later, at age 94, without telling a single soul how she spent it. The only purchase we noticed was when she turned up in church one Sunday morning wearing a new red hat. There was no new roof on the house, no new car, no gift to charity that any of us knew anything about. Just the red hat.

We *did* know one thing she *didn't* spend it on. My mother, after several months of family speculation, got up the nerve to ask, "Did you pay taxes on the money?"

"Of course not," Mama Cooper shot back. "What are they going to do to an old lady? Put me in jail?"

"Yes," said mother. "They might."

But they never did. As far as any of us knew, the tax man never questioned Mama Cooper about her Piggly Wiggly winnings. If he had, I imagine he would have gotten the same kind of defiant reaction as my mother did. I'm sure Mama Cooper faithfully paid taxes on her limited income. But she probably considered the prize money a gift, a reward perhaps for good behavior — something between her and the Lord and Piggly Wiggly.

Now, I certainly don't recommend defiant flaunting of tax laws. But God bless Mama Cooper for a story that gives me a chuckle every April

15th when I mail in my Form 1040 — and every time I eat a peanut butter and banana sandwich.

The Games Southerners Play— Part One

I t is said that in our southern states, college sport is a form of religious expression — football in the Deep South, basketball in the mid-Atlantic. We observe occasions when our favorite teams collide with a gut-wrenching, sweat-soaked fervor that one also associates with snake-handling, foot-washing and speaking in tongues. Especially, speaking in tongues, as in: Gawmighty, lookitat suckarun. If he's our sucka, we experience salvation. If he's the other team's sucka, we feel like Jonah, swallowed by the whale.

My good wife and I were sitting in the Louisiana Superdome some years ago, watching our favorite college football team play Ohio State in the Sugar Bowl. Paulette observed, "A thousand years from now, when archaeologists dig up this place, they'll say that this is where we worshiped." She's a wise and perceptive woman. Our favorite team happened to win that day. We were in a state of grace that bordered on religious transcendence.

These days, we still experience the thrill of victory and the agony of defeat when a team we care about takes the field or court. Paulette and I are a little mellower about it than we used to be — age may have something to do with it — but many of our friends and relatives still worship at the shrine with enthusiasm undiminished.

My late uncle Edd was a perfect example of unbridled sport worship. His favorite team was the Alabama Crimson Tide — football, of course. He thought basketball was something to keep the student body occupied between the bowl game and spring practice. If you are a true and loyal fan of the Crimson Tide, your everlasting arch enemy is anyone who is devoted to the Auburn Tigers. A Tide victory over Auburn on the last Saturday in November ensures Alabama faithfuls a warm and self-righteous winter. A loss brings thoughts of self-immolation.

Uncle Edd never attended Alabama, but he was the school's most devout follower, and the bane of every Auburn fan in the small town where he lived. Auburn's mascot is a magnificent eagle. If Alabama won the game, Uncle Edd would celebrate by hanging dead chickens over the front doors of the Auburn faithful in town, especially the ones who couldn't take a joke.

My own situation is a bit less cut-and-dried. I come from what in Alabama is referred to as a "mixed marriage." My mother attended Alabama. My father played football at Auburn. On the last Saturday of each November, they didn't speak. Sometimes, the silence could last through December, depending on which team won and by how much, and whether the winner's fan in the marriage got a bad case of the smart-mouth.

In my youth, I was an ardent Auburn fan. The Tigers (or War Eagles, as some call them) had great teams during my teenage years, while Alabama fell on hard times. I dreamed of attending

Auburn as a student, but to my great dismay found that the school, at that time, offered no degree in communication. "I don't intend to educate a bunch of disc jockeys," an Auburn president once told me when I suggested the school start such a program. So I swallowed my disappointment and enrolled at Alabama, about the time that the late coach Paul "Bear" Bryant began guiding the Tide to national championships.

I got caught up in the excitement of being on the Alabama campus during what we old-timers now refer to as "the glory years." Who wouldn't? But over time, I've also had a soft spot in my heart for Auburn and I have managed to be a fan of both schools' athletic programs — except, of course, on the last Saturday in November. My Uncle Edd always viewed my divided athletic loyalties with a bit of suspicion. Auburn, I should add, now has a very fine program in communication, and I don't believe all of its graduates are disc jockeys.

Far wiser people than I have observed that in the South, college sport — especially football — has been a form of redemption. During the early part of this century, when the Southern states labored under the burdens of poverty and widespread illiteracy, football exploits became a source of great pride, far beyond the games themselves. If a Southern team whipped a Northern team, it translated into a general feeling of fiercely-defiant we're-okayness. The Civil War was refought on countless Saturday afternoons, and often, the result was different from the original.

Today, you're as likely as not to find the roster of any college athletic team to be a marvelous melting pot of young Americans from every corner of this country and a more-than-fair sprinkling of players from other countries. These young folks aren't fighting the Civil War any more. It's more like the foxholes of World War Two, where boys from Tennessee shared miseries with young fellows from New Jersey and both learned that people are pretty much the same, regardless of where they're from.

Still, we have our loyalties, our agonies and ecstasies, when athletes wearing the colors of our favorite teams take the field or court. Our devotion has its excesses, of course, but the business is pretty much harmless — and, for a few hours on a Saturday afternoon, keeps us out of trouble. Sort of like going to church or synagogue.

The Games Southerners Play— Part Two

I am driving along a narrow two-lane rural road somewhere in the South. My front-seat passenger is from another part of the country. As we pass other vehicles, the drivers, without fail, wave to us.

My passenger is perplexed. "Why are they doing that?"

I explain to my passenger that they wave for one of three reasons: they assume that if you're on this road, you must be from around here or know somebody who is; they assume that you're lost and they sympathize; or they assume that you're neither lost nor from around here, and they feel compelled to play The Game.

College athletic contests define a great deal of what life is about in our Southern states. But Southerners also engage in social gamesmanship with equal devotion and fervor.

A Southerner's favorite social game is "Who are your people?" And by "people," the Southerner means: the vast array of relatives, friends and acquaintances that make up a person's human universe; all of *their* relatives, friends and acquaintances; and anyone else that you or they may be remotely aware of, especially through gossip.

It is the Southerner's primary objective in life — beyond food, shelter and football — to establish some sort of connection with other human beings. It is not enough that I meet you, shake your hand and engage in conversation both trivial and profound. I must find out *who you are.* And that encompasses where you came from and who you know. In other words, who are your people? Assemble any group of Southerners, especially people coming together for the first time, and you will observe this social phenomenon — this joyous game-playing — in its full-blown glory.

Some of it, of course, amounts to snobbery: unless you came from the finest stock, you're not worth knowing. But for most Southerners, it's quite the opposite — an attempt to reach out to another human being on the most elemental level.

Southerners will play the game almost to the point of desperation, grasping at the tiniest glimmer of a connection. Let's say, for instance, that you are from Minnesota, have never been south of Chicago until today, and don't know anyone else who has. I will gnaw at you like a dog worrying a bone until I finally establish that your great-

great-grandfather fought with a Minnesota infan-
try brigade at the Second Battle of Bull Run and
may have exchanged shots with my great-great-
grandfather, who was one of Stonewall Jackson's
North Carolina infantrymen. There, now. We've
established a connection. I know who your people
are. I will not be defeated in this.

I have a friend in another Southern state who
takes this business almost to the extreme. His
hobby is going to funerals. If he is driving along a
narrow two-lane rural road and happens upon a
church where a funeral is in progress, he will stop,
enter, take a seat in the rear, and sit quietly
through the service (even, on occasion, shedding
a circumspect tear for the deceased). He will accompany the mourners to graveside for the inter-
ment. And then he will mingle with the crowd,
playing "Who are you people?" He will work like
the dickens to establish some kinship or acquaintance, however remote. He's usually quick at
making genuine connection in his own Southern
state, where everybody seems to know everybody
else and half the folks are kin to each other. But
he has wandered across the border into neigh-
boring states and enjoyed similar results. If all
else fails, he will make up something. As he de-
parts, I can just hear one of the mourners: "Oh,
you know, that's the boy that went to the Citadel
with second-cousin Irene's neighbor's sister's
youngest child, the one that crash-landed in the
Simpson's pasture back yonder." Oh, that one.

When I tell people who are not from the
South about my funeral-attending friend, I get odd
looks and comments like, "That's truly strange."
But my friend is simply the fringe expression of a
basic, native Southern impulse: *I am prepared to
like you and would be honored to be your friend,*

but first we must establish some basis upon which to take that leap of faith upon which all friendships depend.

Durham novelist Reynolds Price says that in the South, our families are our entertainment. As a lifelong Southerner, Mr. Price knows that we stretch the concept of "family" to its utter limits when we play "Who are your people?" We are all each other's people here.

The quintessential Southern social occasion involves two strangers who sit next to each other at a college football game. By the end of the first quarter, they will have satisfactorily completed a game of "Who are your people?" By halftime, if their team loyalties lie on opposite sides of the line of scrimmage, they will have come to blows.

Two Sure Signs of Southern Summer

Want to know when it's officially summer in the South? Watch for the signs appearing in front of churches, announcing the dates for Vacation Bible School. And watch for fresh okra in the grocery stores. Either is a blessed event. Together, they make my heart sing.

When I was growing up, every kid of every religious denomination went to every Vacation Bible School in our town. We made the rounds of the churches — a week here, two weeks there — and the churches cooperated by not scheduling any conflicts. It was blessed relief for our mothers, who after all ran the churches. They sent fruit punch and Ritz crackers for mid-morning snack time, and a few of them were brave enough to be Vacation Bible School teachers. Most tried to conduct themselves with Christian aplomb. But it helped to have one among the faculty like Miz Althea Prescott, whom I remember thundering out one day, "The Lord wants everybody to sit down and shut up."

I always thought you were taking your life in your own hands when you let a bunch of younguns out of school for the summer and then tried to make them behave at Vacation Bible School. It was mostly organized chaos. Like when we built birdhouses at the Baptist Church and tacked one young fellow's pants to his chair.

The first time I was ever on television was at Vacation Bible School. My best friend Booger and I were among the older kids that year, and we came up with the bright idea of staging a religious TV show in the church sanctuary. We made cameras out of cardboard boxes and microphones out of toilet paper rolls and organized the little kids into a series of song-and-dance acts, all with Biblical themes. The teachers thought it was all real cute until I came on with the commercial. For Casey Coffins. From the wings came two hefty boys dragging a pine box with another kid inside. As I waxed eloquent about entering the hereafter in a Casey Deluxe Model, the coffin occupant sat up and waved gaily to the sanctuary crowd. It took awhile for the teachers to restore order. We could tell who the really cool parents in the audience were. They were the ones who laughed.

Since I'm now too old to attend Vacation Bible School, I have to content myself with okra.

In my mind, it is also a religious experience.

Okra is the queen of vegetables — elegant without being overbearing. It is first of all an efficient food. Like shrimp, you snip off both ends and eat everything that's left. It is also a simple food. I dare say you will not find recipes in your cookbook for "okra flambe," "okra quiche" or "okra Rockefeller." You don't have to worry about whether to serve white wine or red. The proper way to serve okra is with iced tea or buttermilk.

I am partial to fried okra, dipped in a little egg batter and corn meal and popped into a pan or deep fat fryer. (I hope my doctor isn't reading this.) But I have also on occasion enjoyed boiled okra. The late poet laureate of the rural South, Brother Dave Gardner, spoke lyrically of "stewed okra and tomatoes on light bread, so thick you have to lift and eat fast, lest it fall through the middle." It was such thoughts that made Brother Dave say, "Rejoice, dear hearts!"

The only trouble with boiled okra is that it is a world of trouble to eat. You can chase it around your plate for most of the dinner hour before you finally corner it against your biscuit. When my friend Delbert Earle has boiled okra for dinner, he simply lumps everything together in one pile – okra, field peas, sliced ham and potato salad. Each mouthful a potpourri.

Not every year is a good year for okra. Let a drought come along, and the supply is reduced to a dribble. And that's a summer when we okra lovers suffer true deprivation. But when we have a fine season, we make regular joyous pilgrimages to our local farmers' markets for some of the home-grown stuff. Oh, rapture!

If you see a fellow walking along with a big grin on his face during a Southern summer, it's not because he won the lottery. It's because he just had a fine mess of okra for dinner.

If you see a dear lady who looks a little shell-shocked, it may be because she is laboring for the Lord at Vacation Bible School. She has a special place reserved for her in heaven. Next summer, she may opt for manual labor. For the present, offer her a little sympathy. And maybe some okra.

Games of Chance, Games of Folly

I have had two close encounters with gambling during my lifetime and lived to tell about it. I shall relate them to you.

The first was in 1963, when I was a student at the University of Alabama. I entered my fraternity house one early September afternoon, just before fall classes were to begin, to find a poker game underway. I was invited to join, but since I had just put a dollar's worth of gasoline in my car, I was broke and had to decline. I did observe, however. The game they were playing was called Anaconda. The rules appeared to be intricate and exotic and the action was very fast. It started with modest stakes, but things soon escalated. Large sums changed hands. And in short order, one of my good friends had lost his tuition and expense money for the semester.

I must say that he took it like a man, without whining and complaining. He stayed around campus all that fall, supporting himself with odd jobs and the charity of his friends and trying to figure out what to tell his folks. At the end of the semester, when the university sent home grade reports to all the parents, his got none. He was forced to confess his sins and was brought home to spend the rest of the school year in manual labor in the family construction business. He returned to school the next fall a wiser fellow, and henceforth avoided Anaconda.

Six years later, in 1969, I was a member of the Alabama National Guard and was invited to join my fellows for two weeks of summer fun at Camp Shelby, Mississippi — a sun-blasted expanse of sand, pine trees, chiggers and rattlesnakes near Hattiesburg. As a young lieutenant, I was billeted in the Officers' Compound, one room of which was cleared of its usual furnishings to make way for a large round poker table with chairs. Every evening, a number of the officers and gentlemen gathered around the table and wagered large sums of money on card games. I was invited to join, but on a lowly lieutenant's salary, I could scarcely afford the opening ante. I declined, but spent most nights observing. It was high entertainment, lubricated by various fermented spirits and scintillating conversation. Many lies were told. Much money changed hands.

During the second week of camp, the usual participants began to feel somewhat jaded. Some had gone bust and dropped out of the competition and the rest seemed to just trade what money that was left without a clear champion. What they needed was fresh meat, new blood. And they found it in the person of a Mississippi National Guard major general who was visiting Camp

Shelby. He let slip the information at the Officers' Club that he was a pretty fair poker player. And so he was invited to join the big game.

The general arrived that night in high spirits with a thick roll of bills. He was accompanied by a uniformed aide-de-camp who stood at parade rest in one corner while the general took his seat and proceeded to show those old Alabama boys how to play poker.

The players took turns dealing, and each dealer got to choose the game for that hand — five-card stud, deuces wild, etc. As the night wore on, the games got more and more complex. One in particular I remember was something called "Piccolo Pete with a Tiddle in the Middle and a Tiddle on the End, High-Low." The "tiddles" were opportunities to fatten the pot with greenbacks. The old Alabama boys began to win sizeable sums of the visiting general's money. He got more red-faced by the hour, but manfully struggled on until, about two o'clock in the morning, he rose and bade his hosts good night and he and his aide-de-camp marched smartly out. By that time, the old Alabama boys had relieved him of several thousand dollars.

You will note that in both of the instances I have cited above, I did not lose a red cent. The incidents provided cheap lessons to me. I have never had either the stomach nor the excess funds for games of chance. Moreover, I have come to the conclusion that gambling is to be avoided because it makes no sense, either as an individual pursuit or as public policy. Especially as public policy.

Thus, I was delighted when gambling as public policy suffered two major southern setbacks. The South Carolina Supreme Court put an end to video poker in that state. And voters in Alabama resoundingly defeated a referendum that would have set up a state lottery. The year before the South Carolina court decision, citizens of that state pumped $2.8 billion dollars into poker machines, as much as they spent on groceries. Most of the players got results similar to those of my college friend and that Mississippi general. The same holds true for folks who buy lottery tickets. If they want to be bamboozled, okay. But state governments ought not to be involved in such.

Next time you hear a legislator or other state official talk about gambling as public policy, see if you can arrange for him or her to sit in on a high stakes poker game. An evening of Anaconda or "Piccolo Pete with a Tiddle in the Middle, and a Tiddle on the End, High-Low" can be a powerful curative.

Dog Days Remind Me of Boots

When we enter what's called the dog days of summer, that sultry, sticky period when sails droop, people wilt, and dogs look for shade under the nandina bush, my thoughts inevitably turn to — well — dogs. Summer, especially in its doldrums, is made for a boy and a dog, especially in a small Southern river town where heat phantoms hover above the pavement and your bicycle seat gets so hot you can't sit on it and the imagination drifts across long, lazy afternoons interrupted only by an occasional thunderstorm.

Her name was Boots and she was a singular dog in only one respect — she was mine. Her mother was a purebred Boxer. Her father? Well, he could have been any of a hundred undistinguished mutts in Elba, Alabama. Or he could have been all of them. Boots was a true descendant of the town's entire dog population. Her mother was a fun-loving gal, and I believe Boots inherited much of that free spirit. I got her as a puppy, and of course shared her with my three siblings. But being the oldest, I took on the responsibility of her care and discipline. I cared about her a lot. I disciplined her not at all. We got along famously. She was, in short, my dog.

Boots had her charming eccentricities. She loved to swing in the front porch swing, drink soda pop, and eat watermelon. She especially liked the swing. She would start at one end of the porch, race to the other end, fling herself into the swing, and start it swinging. She would lie there, nodding in near-sleep, until the "cat died," then go do it again, over and over for hours. Sometimes we would gather the neighborhood kids just to watch her perform. She was equally adept at watermelon eating, though she never did learn to spit out the seeds. I had to prepare the slices for her. The look on her face as she chewed was pure joy, especially if she could wash down the watermelon with soda pop.

Boots was a religious dog. My family attended Elba Methodist faithfully — Sunday School, morning and evening worship services, Youth Fellowship, and Wednesday Prayer Meeting. Boots always accompanied us and slept the sleep of the righteous outside the front door of the church until we emerged. When we would go to the beach for a week in the summer and leave Boots behind in Elba, she would attend church without us. She somehow knew when it was Wednesday and Sunday.

Boots was also an aquatic dog. We had a fine public swimming pool in Elba, into which the likes of Boots were not allowed. She would accompany us to the pool and sit longingly outside the fence while we cavorted in the water. There were no such restrictions on the Pea River, where my friends and I spent a good deal of time. When we borrowed somebody's old rowboat and went fishing, Boots dog-paddled along behind until she tired, and then we hoisted her into the boat where she sat at the bow, keeping a lookout for rhinoceros and crocodiles.

Boots was allowed privileges that other local dogs were not. She was, to my knowledge, the only dog to accompany our Boy Scout troop on a camping trip. It was her only trip with the troop, because she helped herself to some hot dogs intended for the enjoyment of the entire group. As Boots' host and closest friend, I was not the most popular guy in camp that trip.

Boots was a boy's dog, and she spoiled me as far as dogs are concerned. None of the dogs that have passed through my life since has held a candle to her.

There was Rebel, who was a mascot of my fraternity at the University of Alabama, a school noted in the early '60s for its party atmosphere. Some of my fraternity brothers introduced Rebel to the demon rum — starting with beer and working up to the hard stuff. Rebel became an alcoholic and on Sunday mornings, after a Saturday night frat party, had the worst head in the house.

There was Rover, acquired by my dear wife Paulette shortly after we married. I was working the night shift at a Montgomery television station, and Paulette's primary evening activity was spoiling Rover. He was, to use one of our older daughter's favorite expressions, "out of hand." Rover loved to ride in the car, but since he had a bad habit of scratching the dashboard, I banished him. When we would get ready to go somewhere, Rover would spreadeagle himself on the top of the car and ride all over Montgomery that way. I was known in town as "That TV Guy with the Crazy Dog." Rover ate holes in the bedspread and a good bit of the back porch screen door, and finally he ate a good bit of a neighbor.

And then there was Bojangles, a gift from my mother-in-law, who endeared himself to all by growling over his food and then taking a nip at the baby.

We haven't had a dog for about twenty years or so. If there were another Boots somewhere, I might consider it. But then, Boots inhabited a special time and place. I'm content with the memory of it, and her.

Did You Hear the One About the Politician...?

I was musing on the idea of Southern politicians, and I came to the same conclusion you probably did some time ago: they just aren't what they used to be. The history of Southern politics in this century is a rogue's gallery of charmers, rapscallions, crooks and con artists, with an occasional statesman thrown in. It has been my pleasure over the years to have known some of them and to have heard stories about a good number of others. Like the politicians themselves, the stories are larger than life. I hereby recount three for your entertainment.

Big Jim and the Aircraft Carrier

Some of my favorite Southern politician stories concern the late James Elisha "Big Jim" Folsom of Alabama, who stood about six-feet-seven and had a prodigious capacity for the fermented fruit of the grape.

Big Jim once hosted a meeting of the Southern Governors Conference at Point Clear, across the bay from Mobile. He was anxious to make a good impression on his fellow chief executives and their ladies and staffs, so he laid on lavish parties, tours and entertainments, among which was a cruise aboard a United States Navy aircraft carrier based nearby at Pensacola, Florida.

The story goes that Big Jim rose early on the day of the cruise and began to drink his breakfast. By the time the entourage arrived at

Pensacola, he was in superb form. "Skipper, y'all gonna give us a good show?" he kept inquiring of the carrier's captain. The captain assured him repeatedly that it would indeed be a performance that the governors would long remember.

The aircraft carrier steamed out of Pensacola into the Gulf of Mexico with Big Jim lurching about the bridge and keeping the heat on the captain. The carrier finally turned into the wind and got ready to launch its planes as the gubernatorial gathering looked on eagerly from the best seats in the house. The first plane revved its engine and was catapulted down the deck and into the air, whereupon its engine promptly stalled and the craft pancaked into the Gulf. Alarm bells and claxons sounded and the ship erupted into general pandemonium. The pilot climbed out onto the wing and waved to let everyone know he wasn't hurt, then leaped into the water as the plane began to sink. Big Jim looked on, wide-eyed, then turned to the captain and slapped him on the back with a roar. "By God cap'n, if that ain't a good show, I'll kiss your a—!"

Billy and the Fire Truck

Some of the most colorful characters in Southern politics over the years have been, not the officeholders themselves, but their kinfolks. And there is probably none more so than Billy Carter of Plains, Georgia, brother of the former president.

I am told that among Billy's innocent vices was a remarkable talent at games of chance, one of which was a regular Saturday night high-stakes poker game in a small town not far from Plains, across the state line in Alabama. Another frequent participant in the game was the mayor of this Alabama town, a man who was not quite so skilled at cards as Billy, but nevertheless a daring soul when it came to wagering.

One Saturday night, so the story goes, Billy was winning a good deal of money, and much of it was coming from the mayor. Then the mayor's luck turned — he drew a fine hand and determined to make up his losses with one fell swoop. Being somewhat short of cash, the mayor bet the town's fire truck. Billy won and drove the fire truck back to Plains. The mayor spent Sunday morning collecting enough money from friends to go to Plains and buy back the truck, which he was able to do before any fires broke out.

The Mayor's Toupee

And finally, there is the tale of a certain Southern governor's race some time back, which pitted an upstate country boy against an urbane, sophisticated mayor of the state's largest city. The country boy, deciding that he was no match for the mayor's brains and *savoir faire*, decided to focus the election on the issue of whether or not the mayor wore a toupee.

The mayor — something of a stuffed shirt — refused to discuss a subject that he considered beside the point and beneath his dignity. So the country boy went on television night after night, asking the electorate: "Is it a hairpiece, or ain't it? The mayor won't say. But have you noticed, when he smiles or frowns, his hair don't move. Now, a fellow who won't shoot straight about his hair won't shoot straight about anything else."

Guess who won.

By the way, I have heard these stories from persons who swear by their veracity, including some who purport to be eyewitnesses. If the tales are not true, they should be.

Growing Up with Private Ryan

More than forty years ago, I discovered World War Two in my grandmother's attic.

The attic was an architectural afterthought, added to my grandparents' home after my hometown flooded in 1929. My grandfather, who was the mayor, wanted to make sure that his family had a high-and-dry refuge if the river ever got up in the town again. So he built the attic — actually, just one big room in the shape of a chunky cross with four large closets tucked into the eaves of the house.

My father and three uncles served in World War Two, and when they came home from overseas, they brought the odds and ends of their experience in duffel bags and trunks and footlockers. Each family was assigned one of those attic closets where they stored away their memorabilia. It was a way, I suppose, of putting the war behind them and getting on with the business of jobs and families and a normal life.

One summer when I was twelve or so, having nothing purposeful to do with the long hours of vacation, I climbed the stairs to the attic room and began to idly rummage about. I found their war in the most personal of expressions — love letters to and from wives and girlfriends, maps of countries I had barely heard about, bits of foreign currency, yellowing photos of pilots and sailors and soldiers, small olive drab cans of military rations — biscuits, powdered milk, and the like.

The most exotic experience of the four men was that of my uncle Bancroft, who had been a P-51 fighter pilot stationed in England but flying missions across the English Channel into France, Belgium and Germany. He and his fellow fly-boys escorted bombers and provided close support to the Allied ground forces after the Normandy invasion. It was harrowing work. On one mission, his plane was crippled by enemy fire and he was forced to bail out over the English Channel, whereupon he was rescued and lived to fight again.

In Bancroft's attic trunk I found a parachute. And in my fevered twelve-year-old imagination, I assumed — hoped — that it was the very parachute that he had used to escape his burning P-51. I climbed out onto the roof with parachute in hand and launched myself into space, discovering as I plummeted into a nandina bush that the parachute was much too small to support a human being. It was, I believe, more properly used for a flare.

The point is, the war came alive for me in the odd fragments of my father's and uncles' lives there in the attic. Sure, I had heard about the war. When I was twelve years old, it had only been over for ten years. But here was the story of the intimate involvement of men I knew and loved, my flesh and blood. They had gone in harm's way because they wanted to protect me and every other American from unspeakable evil.

When I saw the movie "Saving Private Ryan," it all came home to me again. And this time, I was struck by the incredible youth of the men who bled on Omaha Beach and in the fields and villages beyond. I realized that my father and uncles went off to war as boys and were changed into men by the raw, terrible experience of it. Sure, the war altered every aspect of the world as we know it — the geopolitics, the economies, the social structure of entire nations. It was a global cataclysm. But on its most important level, it was a highly personal thing, transacting one young life at a time.

A character in one of my novels says, "War is made by men who are too old and fat to fight, and fought by men who are too young to know better." It's not an anti-war statement, just plain fact. Warriors are young by necessity, for only the young can bear the physical and emotional rigors of combat. The movie, *Saving Private Ryan*, says that in the maelstrom of battle, there is no such thing as victory. If a man survives one fight, there is always another. Always a hill, a bridge, a town, a target just ahead, another promise of pain, exhaustion, death. Then at last someone declares the war is over, and by then, there is no youth left. The war has made old men of even the very young.

Yes, I grew up with Private Ryan. Four of them, in fact. I wish I could have known them as boys. But they left their boyhood in the skies above Europe and Burma, in the cold waters of the English Channel, in the mud of Czechoslovakia. I am stunned and shaken by what Steven Spielberg's movie tells of their experience. I can only look upon them with awe and pay tribute.

The True Boundary of the Deep South

Okay, I know where the Mason-Dixon line is, but there's south and then there's Deep South. And to my mind, the Deep South begins at the state line that divides North and South Carolina.

Folks in other parts of the country may tend to think of the "Carolinas" as a homogeneous region with largely similar geography, populated by largely like-minded people. To a great extent, that's true. But there are differences between the states that Carolinians cherish.

Take geography, for instance. The two Carolinas share a Piedmont, the rolling terrain between mountain and coastal plain that has become the area's economic lifeblood, joined at the hip by that horrifying strip of highway known as Interstate-85 and lined by modern manufacturing plants and research facilities. But then North Carolinians claim true mountains, not just those dinky foothills tucked in the upper left-hand corner of the southern neighbor. And South Carolinians claim the lowcountry, which has more humidity and gentility per square inch than the entire northern state.

Then there's history, which in South Carolina dates from the Civil War. There was no more rabid firebrand in the southern secessionist movement than South Carolina's John C. Calhoun. And it's no accident of fate that the first shot of the war was fired at Charleston. Meanwhile, North Carolina's Governor Zebulon Vance argued forcefully against secession. Once North Carolina voted to join the Confederacy, he became a staunch supporter of the southern cause. But up to that point, he preached reason and unity.

The North didn't forget the difference. When Union general William Tecumseh Sherman set off from Atlanta in the autumn of 1864 on his march across Georgia, he knew that his ultimate target was the Carolinas.

When he reached Savannah and turned north, he vowed to make South Carolina pay for its pre-war rabble rousing. And pay dearly it did. Sherman left a trail of smouldering ruins across the state, including the near-total destruction of Columbia.

North Carolina was a different matter. Sherman — remembering Vance's moderation — largely spared the state. And when the war ended with his forces in occupation of Raleigh, he treated the populace with almost tender-hearted mercy — at least, in comparison with what he had done to South Carolina.

It's my impression that South Carolina's psyche still bears some lingering scars from that long-ago ravaging and that its present-day persona is still partly in league with John C. Calhoun. I'll make a dangerous generalization here and say that South Carolinians are by and large more conservative, more proudly defiant, more protective of their rebellious past than folks in the Old North State. More in concert with their southern neighbors such as Georgia, Alabama and Mississippi. In other words, the Deep South.

If I had any doubts about this, they were recently dispelled by a report on fatback. Or, to be more specific, heart disease. South Carolina, it seems, has a higher death rate from strokes and heart attacks than any state except (guess) Mississippi. The reason, of course, is that Deep South folks cherish their grease and to heck with any-body who tries to take it away from them.

I know whereof I speak. I spent the first twenty-seven years of my life in Alabama, and one of my most indelible memories is that of the annual fish fry fund-raiser at the American Legion post in my hometown. The centerpiece was a vat fashioned from a twenty-gallon oil drum, filled with cooking oil of the most artery-clogging variety and heated by a gas burner to just short of bursting into flame. Into this vat the Legionnaires dropped filleted catfish and globs of cornmeal (hushpuppies), the object being to soak up as much of the artery-clogging grease as possible without burning the food.

As if the fish and hushpuppies weren't enough, the Legionnaires' wives contributed all manner of dessert items. A true Deep South recipe calls for preparation of such a delight with lard.

Had the Legionnaires served side dishes of vegetables, they would all have been cooked with fatback (for the uninformed, chunks of 99-percent pure fat from the back of a hog). The object of cooking with fatback is to suck the nutrition out of, say, a mess of collard greens and replace it with fat globules.

Now, I'm not saying that North Carolinians don't cook this way. Some do. But North Carolina seems to have a larger share of health food nuts than her neighbors to the south — what one writer described as the "runny brie and dry chablis" crowd.

South Carolinians, God love 'em, remain defiantly rebellious in their politics and cooking. They face death bravely every time they sit at table. They eat with gusto and send the bills to their health insurance providers, many of which are headquartered in northern states. It's one more bit of revenge for the burning of Columbia.

My Checkered Past with Tobacco

I smoked a cigar the other day. I know, they're quite the chic thing these days, what with movie stars (not all of them male), peering out at us from magazine covers with stogies in hand. But that's not why I smoked a cigar. And I know they're not good for you. But I smoked it anyway.

This particular cigar was a gift from my daughter, Lee, who bought it in a fine cigar store on one of her summer travels. "It's for a special occasion," she said. So I smoked it when she arrived home from her summer travels. It was a special occasion. I sat on the porch in the good company of Paulette, Lee, and my sister-in-law Cathy, who was visiting us from Birmingham. I prepared myself a light libation and fired up that fine cigar and had a grand old time. For a good while there, I was in a state of grace, which had more to do with the good company than with the cigar. Still, the cigar was a sublime pleasure.

As I smoked, I began to think about my checkered past with tobacco. My first experience was stealing my father's pipe and, with a group of other miscreant boys, smoking a vile substance known as "rabbit tobacco" that we found in a weed-grown lot. We all put on brave faces, but it was not something we yearned to repeat. We went on to other things, like chasing girls.

Then there was my one experience with smokeless tobacco. It was in the spring of my senior year in high school and involved more or less the same group of miscreants, older now but not a whit wiser. One day after lunch, while we were out on the front lawn of the school telling lies and ogling the girls, Wayne Taylor pulled out a pouch of Bull Durham. He offered it around, and not wanting to seem like a wimp, I took a plug and tucked it between my cheek and gum — just like Walt Garrison the football player used to do in the TV ads. I was so busy trying to be cool, I didn't notice that the rest of the guys didn't know any more about chewing tobacco than I did.

We went on to Mrs. Kendrick's English class, and it being a warm day, the windows were all open. For thirty minutes, we took turns trooping to the pencil sharpener and spitting out the window. The girls were all disgusted, but they didn't say anything. Mrs. Kendrick finally did. Tired of all the commotion, she said, "You boys sit down. No more pencil sharpening this period."

We sat. And the longer we sat, the greener we turned. And then one by one, we had to excuse ourselves and make hasty, undignified exits. Bull Durham won, hands down.

In college, I smoked a pipe for awhile. It was just after I heard the French phrase, *savoir faire*. I carried the pipe with me to my first job after college. When the boss saw me light up he said, "If I'd known you smoked a pipe, I'd never have hired you. A fellow can't hold down two jobs at once." It is, I admit, a complicated business. If you've been at it awhile, you have an assortment of pipes and all sorts of instruments with which to operate upon them. The tobacco has to be tamped in just right, or the darn thing will either smoke too much or not at all. You have to know how to hold your mouth just so and say the correct mumbo-jumbo to get it fired up. And there's this nasty-tasting brown liquid that trickles...oh, well, I won't get into that. Anyway, I ditched the pipe.

The only thing I've come across that requires as much work as a pipe is a beard. Common wisdom is that you grow a beard so you don't have to bother with shaving. But a beard must be constantly tended. You have to wash it, comb it, trim it, and inspect frequently for small living things that tend to take up residence in there. I once briefly grew a beard, but abandoned it in frustration the first time I tried to eat barbecued chicken. If you see a man who has a beard *and* smokes a pipe, stay away from him. He's working two full-time jobs already and doesn't have time for you.

That pretty much sums up my experience with tobacco. Oh, I tried cigarettes years ago, but gave them up when I started jogging. So I've been smoke free until that wonderful cigar. I may never smoke another one, and if I do, it will be only for a special occasion — complete with a light libation and good company. Given my past, don't you think that's wise?

The Bermuda Grass Blues

Know what we ought to put on the endangered species list? Teenage lawn mowers. Not the fifteen-year-old Snapper rusting in the garage, but the boys (and occasionally girls) we used to see stalking back and forth across our sunburnt grass on sweltering summer days. Young entrepreneurs who lined up customers in the neighborhood or even across town and mowed the grass every week or so, saving for a used car or college or a trip to the beach.

You still see an occasional teenager mowing a lawn, but chances are he or she is a child of the house, and the lawn mowing falls under the general heading of "chore." Most mowing-for-hire these days is done by professional lawn care services. Their trucks and utility vehicles criss-cross our cities and towns, towing trailers full of expensive equipment — mowers, blowers, edgers, and trimmers. They descend on a lawn like a well-oiled NASCAR crew at a pit stop, and in thirty minutes they turn scraggly grass into manicured beauty. I admire their expertise and efficiency. They are business people, making a decent living at this. But they are not teenage lawn mowers.

I've been there. For several summers as a youth, I had a lawn mowing business. I use the term "business" in the loosest sense. My father was the one who suggested I take it up as a means of gainful summer employment. At the first of each summer, he would advance me just enough money for a down payment on a mower from Western Auto — nothing fancy, just the kind of serviceable homeowner machine you would buy for the occasional trimming of your own estate. I would recruit customers, and when school was out, I would begin a three-month assault on the local grass. It was, I should say, a self-propelled mower. I propelled it myself.

Where I grew up, Bermuda grass grows so thick and so rapidly, domestic animals disappear into it, never to be seen again. My mower groaned and stalled. I sweated and uttered oaths. The heat and humidity were oppressive. Still, I bravely marched on, dragging myself home each night to soak in the tub, eat a morsel, and collapse into bed. At dawn, it began again. Dad offered encouragement. Honest labor, he called it. Learning about the business world.

The pay was middling. Two dollars for the average lawn, three if it included a couple of acres of kudzu vine. I collected cash and stuffed it in my jeans pocket. And every Friday evening when I finished work, I went down to the Western Auto store and made a payment on the mower. I generally had enough left over for a milk shake and a movie.

By the end of the summer I would have the mower paid off. But three months of battling Bermuda grass would have, by that time, reduced the machine to wheezing junk, barely able to cut clover. The next summer, I would start all over again. I repeated this process for perhaps four summers, and I recognize it now for what it was: a scheme by my father to keep me out of trouble. Well, it worked. I had barely enough energy to drink the milkshake, and I fell asleep in the movie.

The summer of my sixteenth year, I wised up. "Time to go down to Western Auto," Dad said in mid-May. "Oh, *contraire*," I replied. "I've got a job as a disc jockey at the radio station."

Throughout that summer, I broadcast the

tops in pops from the air-conditioned comfort of WELB, the Mighty 1320. All my friends listened and called to make requests. I dedicated Johnny Mathis ballads to my sweetheart. I was big cheese. And through the control room window, I watched a poor wretch, a couple of years younger than I, struggle through the Bermuda grass of the station lawn. I mowed our own lawn at home, but that was all. Dad had to buy his own stupid mower.

Don't get me wrong. I don't wish a summer of misery on any teenager. But it's not like it was in the good old days. Modern lawn mowers are truly self-propelled. All the operator need do is follow along at a respectful distance, making neat rows and watching for sticks, rocks and snakes. Kindly homeowners offer cool drinks and fresh-baked cookies. And the pay is astonishing. Twenty-five dollars a lawn is not uncommon, and that's just for the ones without kudzu.

I'd like to see teenage lawn mowing entre-preneurs rise up and reclaim their rightful place in the summer landscape. They'll learn life-alter-ing lessons. After all, look at me. It propelled me into a career in broadcasting. Always, in air-con-ditioned comfort. Always.

Booger and Julius Caesar

B eware, the saying goes, of the Ides of March — the anniversary of the most famous mur-der in literary history. On March 15, 44 B.C., emperor Julius Caesar was slain in the Roman Senate by sixty conspirators. I mark the occasion each year with fond remembrance of my boyhood friend, Booger.

We were best buddies growing up, friends from the time we sat next to each other at Mrs. Brooks' nursery school. We were fellow Methodists, fellow members of a thoroughly inept high school football team, fellow laborers in the vineyards of academe. Booger was true blue, a guy you could count on. His mother was a fantastic cook who always insisted I stay for supper. Plus, he was smart. I hoped some of it would rub off.

Now, about the Ides of March. We were juniors in high school when we were introduced to Shakespeare in Mrs. Ola B. Kendrick's English class. Mrs. Kendrick was determined to bring a little culture into our young lives and lift our thoughts beyond such things as cars, girls, and Elvis Presley. It was a tall order, but she set gamely about the business, as she had done with every junior English class for a good portion of the century. Her vehicle was *Julius Caesar*, highlights of which appeared in our literature text.

Julius Caesar is a ripping good story of angst and intrigue. Caesar was a heckuva dude, a man who conquered Gaul and raided Britain and defeated rivals in a civil war, then took over as emperor. He was magnanimous in victory, pardoning his former enemies and even giving them positions of power in his regime. He probably shouldn't have done that. One of them, Cassius, organized a conspiracy against Caesar and talked Caesar's good friend, Brutus, into joining it. They and fifty-eight other Roman senators stabbed Caesar to death. We thought it was a pretty good mark of Caesar's dudeness that it took sixty guys to kill him.

I think Mrs. Kendrick was pleasantly surprised by our class's interest in the play. What she didn't realize was that we were being influenced by an outside source — the appearance about that time of "Rejoice Dear Hearts," a record album by Southern comedian Brother Dave Gardner, a cut of which was his own hambone version of "Julius Caesar." *Y'all look out for yon Cassius now, y'hear? He hath that lean and hongry look.* Boog and I and just about anyone we knew could recite word for word entire passages from the Brother Dave rendition. They gave delicious texture to Shakespeare's version.

The highlight of the play, as Mrs. Kendrick saw it, was the famous funeral oration given by Caesar's friend and admirer, Mark Antony. You remember the lines from your own school days:

Friends, Romans, countrymen, lend me your ears;

I come to bury Caesar, not to praise him.
The evil that men do lives after them;
The good is oft interred with their bones.

I am quoting from memory here, so don't hold me to an exact wording. The point is that Boog and I and all of our classmates were required to memorize Mark Antony's funeral oration and recite it aloud in front of the whole class, and what I remember of it now, forty years later, is based upon that singular experience.

Boog and I took the assignment seriously. He was a bit shy and nervous in front of an audience. I was appearing on the local radio station at the time, dedicating Elvis Presley tunes to all my friends, and thus more accustomed to, shall we say, public oration. So we studied together, memorized and practiced aloud to each other. He could remember the lines, I could contribute some dramatic flair. Together, we got it down pat.

It went on for days, one after another standing up by the blackboard and doing the Marc Antony bit with varying degrees of success. A few — whether by design or accident — slipped in a little Brother Dave. Boog was the last to recite. When it finally came his turn, he rose confidently, raised one arm in a dramatic gesture, and intoned, "Friends, womans, countrymen..." Then he froze. The class burst into hysterics. It takes very little to get a class of juniors into hysterics. Boog was unable to continue. I think he finally did a private session with Mrs. Kendrick.

Boog went on to become a great orator, quite at home in front of a class. He's an outstanding college professor, though I won't say where because none of his friends there know that his former name was Booger, and I don't want to cause hysterics in a faculty meeting. We lost touch for several years, but now have re-established contact. We exchange books and articles we have written. I mention him often in speeches because he has qualities of character I admire. In adulthood as in youth, he's a man of substance and integrity. True blue, a guy you can count on. If I called him tomorrow and said, "I need you," he would come. I would do the same for him.

I think of Boog often and fondly. Especially on the Ides of March.

Aunt Tootie's Radio

I passed the Pelzer, South Carolina, exit on Interstate 85 and thought about Aunt Tootie and my friend Charles Crutchfield.

The story begins in 1935 with a Chicago-based patent medicine company. They manufactured a wide range of products, including a hair dye called Color-Back and an iron tonic that went by the name of Peruna. The progressive president of the company wanted to advertise his products on this new-fangled contraption called radio, so he called across the country looking for stations that could bring in his kind of audience.

One of his calls was to WBT in Charlotte. "Do you have a hillbilly music program?" the fellow asked.

The station manager turned to young Crutchfield. "Do we have a hillbilly music program?"

"Sure," Crutch fibbed. And then he scrambled to put together a band and get the program on the air. He called the musicians The Briarhoppers, and they took to the WBT airwaves for an hour every afternoon, playing live music, doing corny jokes, and hawking Color-Back and Peruna. Crutch was the announcer, stage manager and general brains behind the operation.

The results were wildly successful. Almost overnight, the Briarhoppers became the biggest radio hit in the Carolinas. When they weren't on the radio, they were doing personal appearances all over the region. Fan mail poured in. And stores had a hard time keeping stocks of Color-Back, Peruna, and the other products of the Chicago company.

That's where Aunt Tootie comes in. She called her nephew Charles Crutchfield on the telephone one day, raving about this new Peruna product. It had changed her life, she said.

"How much of it are you taking?" Crutch asked.

"A bottle a day," she answered. "I'm sleeping better than ever, my appetite is excellent, and I feel wonderful."

What Aunt Tootie didn't know, and what Crutch didn't tell her, was that Peruna was about forty percent alcohol. Dear Aunt Tootie, a teetotaling churchgoing lady, had a constant buzz on.

Aunt Tootie, Peruna, Color Back and Charles Crutchfield have passed on. But in his later years, I spent some marvelous hours with Crutch, hearing stories of his days as a broadcasting pioneer. The story of the Briarhoppers reminded him, and me, of the days when radio was an intensely personal and intimate medium, bringing a ray of sunshine into the bleak Depression-era lives of millions of Americans. Crutch and the other announcers of the era delivered their commercials live. When they promoted a sponsor's business or product, it amounted to a personal endorsement. There were charlatans and hucksters on the radio, of course, but they didn't have the staying power of people like Crutch and the Briarhoppers. The Aunt Tooties of the south came to trust what they said. For Aunt Tootie, Peruna worked.

Radio had changed a lot by the time I came along in the 1950's as a teenage disc jockey on a small-town 1,000 watt station. We played a lot of records on WELB, and a few of the commercials had fancy musical backgrounds and theme songs. But it was still an intimate medium with a lot of what I think of as two-way trust. You had the feeling that listeners were inviting you into their homes and automobiles and that you should act like a gracious guest and not offend. If they came to believe you were on the up-and-up, they would listen to your program and patronize the merchants you advertised. You could, as Crutch and the Briarhoppers did years earlier, bring a little sunshine.

The only sponsors who gave me much pause were the palm readers. Every few months one would pull up in a huge Cadillac in front of the radio station, walk in with a big wad of cash, and pay top dollar for air time. The station manager had a standard spiel. Madame Flora or Sister Carmel would divine the future, plumb the mysteries of life and love, and for an extra five dollars, remove warts. Was this the kind of material we ought to have on the air? I asked. Of course, said the station manager. Lots of folks believe in and patronize palm readers, he said. And for everybody else, it's entertainment. Who were we to deny them the airwaves?

Charles Crutchfield and I bemoaned the current state of programming in American radio, but in truth there are still remnants of what we admire. You find them on small-town stations, often on the AM dial, where you can hear the "Swap Shop" and the "Obituary Column of the Air" and a daily inspirational message. The announcers are people you know and trust.

Next time you're passing through a small town, find the local station and listen for awhile. You'll probably find something you like. So would Aunt Tootie.

Mama Cooper Knew
All About Time

There was a little advertisement in the news paper: LULU HONEYCUTT TURNS 50, DE-MANDS RE-COUNT!

Happy birthday, Lulu. And get a grip. Turning fifty is no big deal. I've been there. Would you rather *not* turn fifty? And what if you got a re-count? You might be sent back to adolescence. Anybody out there want to go through adolescence again? I didn't think so.

I'm one who enjoys birthdays. I even invented a thing called the birth-half-day, which means you get to celebrate twice a year. My daughter, Lee, was born on February 22 and I was born on August 22, so each of us celebrates a birth-half-day on the other's birthday. I haven't convinced people to give me presents on my birth-half-day, but I'm working on that.

I suppose I got my cavalier attitude toward age from my grandmother, Nell Cooper. Whatever age Mama Cooper was, she seemed to enjoy it. She didn't let things like time bother her.

Take, for instance, the great Daylight Savings Time controversy back in the '60s. The legislature in my home state debated fiercely about whether to observe Daylight Savings Time. The Farm Bureau opposed it. A spokesman said with a straight face, "It will confuse the farm animals." A lot of folks were confused about the concept of losing or gaining an hour. But Mama Cooper had a simple solution. During the months when Daylight Savings Time was in effect, she slept an hour later every morning. During the summer, she rose at eight. During the winter, at seven. It worked for her, and she was able to concentrate her mental energies on the truly important things, such as whether to have sweet milk or buttermilk with her supper biscuits.

Mama Cooper's attitude about time extended to human basics. She believed that given time — and a little help — everything that was supposed to work out would work out. One of my indelible memories of boyhood was entering her kitchen door to the smell of prunes cooking in senna leaves. For the uneducated, senna is a powerful laxative. A prune by itself is artillery. A prune cooked in senna is an artillery brigade. If you were feeling "puny," as Mama Cooper put it, or even looked as if you felt puny, she would administer two prunes and a spoonful of juice. Then let time take over. You would stay close to home for several days. You had nothing *but* time.

Mama Cooper's kitchen was a marvelous place, and time was an important ingredient in everything that came out of it. Her recipes were ancient things, time-tested concoctions handed down through generations, everything made from "scratch." During the winter months, when prunes weren't cooking in senna, my favorite aroma at her house was of home-made rolls rising atop the gas space heater in her living room. They took their sweet time, but if you were patient, you were rewarded with a roll so light and fluffy that blackberry jelly fairly floated atop it. Fast food to her was warmed-up leftovers. She was suspicious of things that came out of cans.

One of Mama Cooper's specialties concerned blackberries. In the late summer she would buy gallons of berries and then spend days in the kitchen making jelly, nectar and — just for cooking, of course — a small amount of wine. Everything took time, especially the wine, which had to "work" for days on end. In her later years, Mama Cooper would occasionally get confused about which jar contained non-alcoholic nectar and which wine. One of the relatives would find her pleasantly tipsy, letting time take its own course.

There is something about time that eases human discourse. In my novel *Old Dogs and Children,* one character says to another, "You can't stay mad at somebody when you have to look 'em in the eye every day." That's not universally true. I know people in my hometown who have been mad at each other for years. But mad or not, they still manage to get along, to accommodate each other, warts and all. In a small town, where you keep bumping into the same people day after day for years and years, time forces you to at least be civil. Mostly.

I dedicated *Old Dogs and Children* to Mama Cooper, who knew all about time, about how to make peace with it, to let it be your friend. Obviously, it worked for her. She lived to be 94, and it would never have occurred to her, as it did to Lulu Honeycutt, to demand a re-count.

The last time I saw Mama Cooper, she was bed-ridden in a nursing home. Not an easy way to go. But her spirit was unflagging. She said to me, "Bobby, I've give out but I haven't give up." She never did. She had all the time in the world.

Rescuing Michael Jordan

They're having quite a ruckus these days in Spot, North Carolina. The community has been in an uproar since Clyde Lee Higgins appeared before the town council and urged the honorables *not* to name a street for Michael Jordan, the world's greatest basketball player. The council was all set to change Blue Mold Lane to Michael Jordan Boulevard until Clyde Lee threw a monkey wrench into the works. In the wake of his pronouncement, Spot has become about evenly divided between folks who think Clyde Lee is a meddlesome fool and those who believe he has a point.

For the benefit of those who haven't heard, here's a recitation of the facts:

Folks in Spot have long claimed a connection to Michael Jordan. Since the town is located halfway between Wilmington and Chapel Hill, it stands to reason that Michael would have passed through Spot on his travels between his hometown and the community where he played college ball.

Not only that, citizens well remember the occasion when Dean Smith took the Tarheels to Spot one night during preseason for a benefit scrimmage (though no one seems to remember what the scrimmage benefited). The Town Council had renamed the high school gymnasium as the Spot Coliseum in honor of the occasion though, unfortunately, the roof repairs had not been completed. The Tar Heels had to dribble around puddles when the thunderstorm hit just after halftime, but the *Spot Free Press* reported that a capacity crowd of three hundred witnessed a spirited game, won by the Michael Jordan-led Blues. The *Free Press* article had a brief quote from Michael, who reportedly turned to a teammate as they left the court at game's end and said, "Can you believe this place?" Spoteans took that as a high compliment.

So when Michael Jordan announced his retirement from the NBA, folks in Spot began to cast around for some way to honor him and fittingly memorialize his long association with the community. It was Mayor Briggs who came up with the idea of Michael Jordan Boulevard, and the idea caught on like perfumed soap at a foot-washing. The Ladies of Petunia garden club drew up plans for beds of flowering perennials to be placed at either end of the street along with appropriate signs. The editor of the *Spot Free Press* began selling advertising for a commemorative issue. A committee of Rotarians, scout leaders and fire department officials began preparations for a parade and dedication ceremony. Mayor Briggs alerted the Raleigh news media of an impending announcement of some importance.

Then just as the Spot town council was about to formally vote the name change, Clyde Lee showed up and raised the issue of the Buster Boudreaux affair.

Buster Boudreaux, as Clyde Lee reminded the honorables, had lived quietly and unobtrusively in a town not far from Spot until the Saturday he went to Raleigh with his wife to shop for curtains. Buster was minding his own business, sitting on a bench outside a department store at Crabtree Valley Mall, when he was approached by a fellow with a clipboard. The fellow said he was looking for some ordinary folks to be contestants on the "Wheel of Fortune" TV game show. And, to hear

Clyde Lee tell it, there are few people in the world more ordinary than Buster Boudreaux.

Buster went to Hollywood and got lucky picking vowels and won some money. The folks back in his hometown watched and cheered, and by the time Buster got back home, he was the biggest celebrity going. In fact, he was the only person in his hometown who had ever done anything remotely famous, unless you count that fellow on Death Row. So the town council named a street for him: Buster Boudreaux Boulevard.

As Clyde Lee described it to the Spot honorables, Buster Boudreaux Boulevard wasn't much of a boulevard — a two-lane street a couple of blocks long, lined with modest homes, a convenience store and a garage. Nothing much had happened along this street for years until they named it for Buster. But with its new name it attracted considerably more traffic than usual, since folks like to be associated with a celebrity. Over the first winter, the street developed some industrial-size potholes and the garage began to do a banner business in front-end alignment. A bootlegger moved into one of the houses and the convenience store started renting out video movies, some of which were of questionable taste.

All of this activity led to even more traffic, especially in the early evenings. Folks would drive by Buster Boudreaux Boulevard to pick up some entertainment of various sorts, hit the potholes, and leave mad.

Neighbors were divided by the turn of events. Some began to fight in their yards. The cops were out there all the time. People began to complain to the town council, which formed a committee to study the situation. The committee studied at great length. So without any official action, folks did the natural thing. They began to call Buster Boudreaux. After all, they said, it was his name on the street, and none of the controversy existed before Buster got, as one matron put it, "high and mighty." Things got progressively worse. His wife was snubbed by a group of ladies in the produce section at the Winn-Dixie and his children were accosted at school.

As Clyde Lee tells it, Buster became desperate. He appeared before the town council and asked them to take his name off the street. While a committee studied that at length, he got an unlisted phone number. Instead of calling to complain, folks went by his house. He eventually sold and moved to Virginia where, as Clyde Lee reports, he lives under an assumed name.

Well, as Mayor Briggs puts it, things have been "put in abeyance" in Spot in regards to the Michael Jordan business. Clyde Lee has raised the spectre of potential scandal and accompanying public unrest. Some local folks think it's much ado about nothing. But others fear that naming a street for Michael might lead to a sullying of their town's reputation statewide. Not to speak of what it might do to Michael.

Clyde Lee has suggested a possible compromise, which the council is expected to form a committee to study. Clyde Lee says they should erect a sign at the city limits which would remind folks of their connection with Michael Jordan without running the risk of another Buster Boudreaux-type fiasco. The sign would read: "SPOT, NORTH CAROLINA. 'CAN YOU BELIEVE THIS PLACE?'"

The council has scheduled a public hearing for next Wednesday night at seven, in case you're interested.

A Detour Named Crawfordville

I f Dwight D. Eisenhower were around today, I'd invite him to visit Crawfordville, Georgia, to see what he wrought. One of the enduring legacies of Ike's eight years in the White House is our interstate highway system. And Crawfordville is one of its victims.

I came to know Crawfordville in 1988 when it served as the location for a motion picture based on my novel, *Home Fires Burning.* Paulette and I spent several days there, watching talented actors bring my imagination to life and getting to know some nice local folk.

Crawfordville's early claim to fame was as the home of Alexander Stephens, the vice-president of the Confederacy. Stephens' birthplace is preserved there as part of a state park and historical site. The main street is part of U.S. Highway 278, which runs through rolling countryside between Augusta and Atlanta. For much of its existence, the highway made the town a thriving place. A constant stream of traffic rumbled through, and many stopped for lunch at Bonner's Café, where the blue plate special consisted of a meat, three vegetables, hot rolls, all the iced tea you could drink, and a slice of lemon meringue pie. And since Crawfordville is the seat of Taliaferro County government, it enjoyed the commerce of country folk who came to town to do business at the courthouse.

And then came Interstate 20, completed sometime in the past couple of decades to connect Augusta and Atlanta. It runs parallel to U.S. 278 — gleaming twin ribbons of concrete upon which you can drive 70 miles an hour (if you want to be legal, most don't) without ever glimpsing a traffic light. People stopped using U.S. 278 unless they had local business, were scared of the interstate, or got lost. Crawfordville the town withered into Crawfordville the movie set. Filmmakers came because they could turn the empty storefronts into anything — a café, a newspaper office, a bank, a barber shop.

One elderly gentleman I met on the main street during my time there told me proudly that Crawfordville had become "L.A. East." By then, it had been the location for several movies. "The last one," he said, "musta been a porno flick. They was riding horses naked over in the park." Oh well, with movies you get some strange stuff.

On a trip awhile back, Paulette and I made a detour off I-20 to Crawfordville. It hadn't changed much since we were there in 1988. We talked with a nice lady who works at Ellington's Dry Goods, one of the few remaining viable businesses. She told us with pride that the town has been the location for eight or nine movies over the years.

Each time the filmmakers come, it's a nice shot in the arm economically and a boost to the town's esteem. You can wander down to the main street and watch famous folks make magic. Maybe even get an autograph or a photo if you're lucky. But the problem with movie folk is that they create a make-believe world of bright lights and celebrity glamour for a few weeks, then they pack up and go home. And when the cameras and actors and scurrying crew depart, the town returns to its sad emptiness.

Bonner's Café still opens for a couple of hours at mid-day and an occasional soul wanders into the courthouse. But mostly, Crawfordville just lives on memory, waiting for the next movie crew to come along and turn those empty store fronts temporarily into the kinds of businesses Crawfordville used to have — before the interstate.

When President Eisenhower came up with the idea of the interstate highway system, he was concerned about the threat of nuclear war. If a foe started dropping bombs on our cities, Ike wanted a system of high-speed, high-capacity highways, something on the order of the German autobahns, to evacuate Americans from trouble.

The system started modestly, with a few key roadways connecting major cities. But over the years, Congress and state legislatures expanded it into the network we have now. And all over America there are hundreds, perhaps thousands of Crawfordvilles — towns the interstates bypassed. Towns that time, hurrying toward the future, has forgotten.

Newly-placed blue and white signs along the shoulders of our superhighways proclaim the "Eisenhower Interstate System." Ike would probably marvel at how efficient the system is, how it has transformed our economy and our culture. But if he could see Crawfordville and its fellow victims, I think he'd be disappointed. A fellow who grew up in small-town Abilene, Kansas, surely cherished the charm and vitality of a bustling, close-knit community. The kind Crawfordville used to be. Before the interstate.

Peanuts, Turbulence and the Bull Bill

S ome years ago, I was on an airliner with then-governor Lester Maddox of Georgia, flying from Atlanta to Los Angeles. As the plane passed over Mississippi, we suddenly hit a pocket of air turbulence. The plane bounced violently. Governor Maddox turned to his traveling companion, a fellow Southern governor, and said, "Hmmm. The legislature must be in session down there." I laughed. Neither of the governors did.

When legislatures meet, some good may result, along with considerable folly. As Will Rogers used to say, "No man's life nor liberty is safe when the legislature's in session."

I had my first exposure to a state deliberative body when I was in junior high school. Our civics teacher took us to Montgomery to observe the Alabama Legislature in session. She had prepared us thoroughly with lectures on the bicameral system, the steps in consideration and passage of bills, and the vital role our citizen representatives played in the business of democracy.

We all trooped quietly into the balcony of the State Senate chamber, awed by the surroundings and the thought of watching history being made. We were greeted by a steady rustling and crackling sound. We looked down to see the senators eating peanuts and throwing the hulls on the floor. We students came from homes where our mothers would kill us if we did that.

One senator was droning at a microphone, elbow propped on a huge truck tire. He was discoursing at great length — not on truck tires, but on the price of fertilizer.

"What's he doing?" one student asked our teacher.

"Filibustering," she answered.

"What's that?"

"That's where they talk all day about nothing to keep from doing any work."

It remains the best definition of a filibuster I've ever heard.

We learned later that the filibustering senator was trying to block passage of a bill that would have imposed a minuscule tax on farm fuel, with the proceeds going to the public schools. The filibuster succeeded. At the end of the day, when the peanuts ran out, the Honorables gave up in bored exhaustion and adjourned to a nearby watering hole to consider their arduous and inspiring work. Farmers continued to ride tax-free. The public schools got by for another year on textbooks from our parents' era.

Several years later, as a young journalist, I found the Alabama Legislature a fascinating story to cover and a microcosm of the human comedy. Peanuts and filibusters were still staples of the legislative diet. Lobbyists prowled the back halls, striking deals and concocting intrigues. The House and Senate were full of colorful characters who clashed by day and drank together by night. Some commendable programs were passed into law. But much of it was like watching a wreck happen.

During one long summer, much of the Honorables' attention and collective wisdom were focused on a bull. Literally, a real live bull. Over at Auburn University, doctors in the veterinary medicine school were getting ready to operate on a prize bull named Lindertis Evulse. Lindertis was a magnificent and expensive beast, but sadly impotent. As the doctors prepared Lindertis for what they hoped would be corrective surgery, the legislature went through a frenzy of resolution-passing, all in the name of wishing Lindertis a successful operation and quick recovery to virile health. Much of the wording of the resolutions bordered on bawdiness. Imagine what flights of eloquence a group of legislators might rise to, presented with the subject of an impotent bull.

Alas, Lindertis's operation failed. He lived out his days in tranquil uselessness. I hope he never knew what a tacky spectacle the legislature had made of his private agony.

When I moved to the Carolinas, I hoped that our legislatures would be more serious about their conduct of the affairs of state. And then the South Carolina legislature spent much of an entire session debating the designation of a "State Dog." I don't remember what breed they finally chose, but the exercise was played out with great jollity by the Honorables in Columbia.

So, legislatures have been something of a disappointment to me. I only take solace in the fact that when they spend their time eating peanuts, filibustering, and considering dog and bull bills, they are at least not involved in such mischief as raising taxes.

While your state legislature is in session, read your local paper diligently and remain informed about the issues, great and small, which your Honorables are considering. But you might want to avoid the airspace over those cities. And visit the legislative halls at your own peril. Legislation is a lot like sausage: you appreciate it a lot more if you don't watch it being made.

What It Was, Was Football

Every time I watch a Super Bowl on TV, I am struck by the skill and athletic grace of the players. I am reminded of my own brief moment of football glory. And I shudder.

In my youth, I was slight of build and somewhat timid of heart, not at all keen on being bashed about the head and shoulders. But my father had been a college football player, and as young men will do to impress their fathers, I decided one year in high school to go out for football.

I was, to put it bluntly, the most inept member of a football team for whom ineptitude was a religion. The year I played, the Elba High Tigers won one game and lost nine. The only team we defeated was Florala High, where football was a non-event. They lost all ten of their games that year. Florala had bigger boys toting tubas in the marching band than they had on the football team.

Coach McCurley called our team together the week before the Florala game, which was to be Homecoming at Elba High. "Boys," he said, "we've got to win this game. The governor is coming." The governor of the state was an alumnus of Elba High, and he would be returning on Friday night for his class reunion. Well, we practiced like demons all week. And on Friday, we thrashed Florala 7-6, only to learn later that the governor, a fellow who would take a nip, was about three sheets to the wind in the stands, and hadn't the foggiest idea what was happening on the field. It was that kind of season.

I was too small to be a tackle, guard or center and too slow to play in the backfield. So Coach McCurley decreed that my position would be end.

Mostly, my position was bench. I played sparingly during that terrible season, usually inserted in the last quarter of games in which the opponent was ahead by more than forty points.

On offense, passes bounced off my helmet. *Look out, Bobby! Huh? BOING!* On defense, I added an element of farce to a line that was already as porous as sand. I lined up alongside my best friend Booger, a massive tackle. During one miserable game, Coach McCurley yelled out to the field, "Bobby and Booger, if y'all ain't gonna tackle 'em, at least wave at 'em so the backs'll know they're coming."

The next season, both Coach McCurley and I gave the Tigers a break. He quit coaching and I quit playing. I think my father was somewhat relieved. I went out for track, which was mostly a non-event at Elba High. I became a fairly decent distance runner. It wasn't hard to get motivated. I pretended that opposing football players were chasing me.

My two younger brothers became stellar football players and redeemed the family gridiron honor. Joel was an all-conference tackle and went on to play college ball. David was such a hard-hitting linebacker that he was known as "The Eraser" long before Arnold Swarzenegger showed up.

The Tigers became a powerhouse over the years. Several players got college scholarships. The team won two state championships. At my own class reunion six years ago, my classmates and I sat in the stands at Homecoming and watched the current team demolish the visitors. They were a fearsome bunch. Not a single pass bounced off anybody's helmet. The modern-day Bobbys and Boogers made tackles at the line of scrimmage.

We old codgers looked at each other, remembered our sad history, and laughed.

In the days since I attempted to play football, it has become mostly a game of giants, even in high school. The mayhem level is incredible. Thank goodness soccer came along for kids who are slight of frame. It's a shame we didn't have soccer at Elba High when I was there. In soccer, it's okay if the ball hits you in the head. *Look out, Bobby! Huh? BOING! Great play!*

I have managed to make at least some use of my brief, checkered football career. A writer never throws anything away. So the hero of one of my novels is a rail-thin sixteen-year-old boy whose father is a 300-pound former college football player. At one point, the youngster says to his father, "I think I'll go out for football." And his father looks him up and down and says, "They'll kill you."

I wish my father had said that to me. It would have saved us all a lot of embarrassment.

Christmas Is for Storytellers

I am a storyteller, and I owe a lot of it to Christmas afternoon at Mama Cooper's house.

In my childhood I was blessed with a large extended family, all of them residents of our small southern town. My grandfather, Bob Cooper, had been a wealthy lumberman in the years before his death in 1929. But by the time I came along, the family's legacy had been reduced to middle-class respectability. Among his four children, one was the postmaster, another was a rural mail carrier, a third was a doctor. My mother, the only daughter, was a schoolteacher married to a civil servant. None of us were wealthy or particularly prominent, but we were large and sometimes boisterous and we were great storytellers. At least, the adults were.

My grandmother, Nell Cooper, was in her seventies when I was a boy. She still lived in the rambling white frame house Bob Cooper had built for her when they were newlyweds. It had sagged with age, along with the family's fortunes, but it still put up a brave front along Claxton Avenue, and it was still the family gathering place. Especially on Christmas afternoon.

It made Christmas as extended as the family. There was the long period of delicious anticipation leading up to the Big Day. Then Christmas morning. And when all the presents were opened and the living room strewn with paper and you were just about to be hit with the inevitable letdown, you remembered Christmas afternoon. All the Coopers and Inmans, the whole brawling crowd of us — nine adults and fourteen children — at Mama Cooper's house.

There were presents. It was the time when Mama Cooper gave her small, carefully-selected gifts to the aunts and uncles. We cousins had drawn names a week before, with a two-dollar limit on the items we exchanged — a month's supply of Lifesavers, caps for the cap pistol you had received that morning from Santa, perhaps a slingshot that made your parents cringe.

The afternoon began with a noisy general visit with all of us packed into Mama Cooper's parlor, then the gifts, then food, all of it prepared by the hostess the week before in her tiny kitchen — lane cake, fruit cake, pecan roll, divinity and fudge. After that, with all the kids as high as a kite on sugar, we were supposed to go outside and play. But I liked to linger behind and secret myself in a corner of the parlor while the adults gathered around the kitchen table in the next room.

There were two items on the menu: egg nog and talk. Mama Cooper was a teetotaling Methodist preacher's daughter, but she allowed alcohol to be consumed in her house this one time during the year. With each succeeding cup of egg nog, the talk got better. Inevitably, it got around to telling stories on each other. It was where I learned family history, myth and lore, all of it filtered through memory.

Much of it was about the Big War. The men had all served in World War Two, and all of them had married and begun fathering offspring either during the war or just after. I didn't know much about the war itself, but I was struck, as I listened to their stories, about the incredible impact it had made on their lives — not the battles so much as the experience of being far from home, seeing strange places, being young and sometimes foolish in a time when the world was turned upside down. For the women back home, it was equally life-altering — the constant worry, the hardships, the aloneness. When the war was over, the boys all came safely home to make mostly quiet lives and raise families. But after what they had all been through, they were a generation for whom nothing could ever be quite the same.

So, they told the stories. I eavesdropped and stored it all away in my own memory. In listening, I came to know how, in the South, families are both our entertainment and our essential bridge across time and space.

Over the years, I have written my own stories. My second novel, in particular, drew heavily on the human drama that I heard around Mama Cooper's table on Christmas afternoon. I published the book with some trepidation and sent copies to all my kin. One uncle wrote back to say, "You got it right." And I believe he meant not so much the detail as the essential meaning of those lives. It was the kindest praise of all.

One Last Journey, with a Little Respect

They had a row awhile back over funeral processions in Mobile, Alabama — a tacky public disagreement in what I've always considered one of the South's more genteel cities. When I think of Mobile, I think of liveoak trees dripping with Spanish moss, azaleas in bloom at Bellingrath Gardens, and gracious old homes presided over by generations of gracious old families. I also think of good manners, which in my book calls for stopping whatever you're doing when a funeral procession passes by. If you're too busy to stop for a funeral procession, you're just too busy. But Mobile's gentility apparently got overtaken by its busyness.

The story in the Mobile paper said many of its readers bemoaned a lack of funeral procession courtesy by local drivers, suggesting that even in the South, polite society is a thing of the past. One local funeral director said, "Everybody's in a hurry to do nothing, to go nowhere." One reader said she saw an 18-wheeler cut into a funeral procession to get to an intersection. Others said when they pull over to let a funeral procession pass, they're the object of obscenity-spewing horn-honkers.

The police used to be a big help, stopping traffic at intersections, waving drivers to the side when the procession approached. But in many places, especially the larger ones, police officers no longer provide escorts for funeral processions. Mobile stopped the practice some years ago, except when the deceased is someone particularly notable.

My, how things have changed.

When I was growing up in a small town not terribly far from Mobile, practically everybody was *in* the funeral procession. But those who weren't invariably stopped to pay their respects, and they didn't need the police department to tell them so. Men standing on the sidewalk removed their hats. Kids stopped their play. Even Ibelle Whitman's old hound dog would raise up from his slumber in front of Whitman's Drug Store as the funeral procession rolled around the town square. Without fail, there went somebody you knew.

Funerals are an essential part of the Southern experience. All sorts of customs grow up around them. One has to do with food, which begins arriving at the home of the deceased shortly after the moment of death, even if the death has been unexpected. It's as if every matron has at least one funeral dish always prepared and ready for delivery. The variety is equally as astonishing as the amount — casseroles, platters of every imaginable meat, cakes and pies, relishes and jellies, gallons of iced tea, urns of coffee. There is never too much of one thing and not enough of another. The women of the community have a collective sixth sense about what to bring and in what quantities, and when to bring it. Such are the mysterious ways of Southern ladies.

Their food is one thing, their presence is another. They work in shifts at the home of the bereaved, serving mounds of food, washing dishes. The community eats its way through the period of mourning. The food is not the important thing, of course, it's the expression of giving. You may not always know the right thing to say, but you always know the right thing to bring.

Other funeral customs are more specific, such as the New Orleans tailgate tradition. Used to be, when an old jazzman died, his fellow musicians would sit on the tailgate of the wagon drawing the casket to the cemetery and play his favorite tunes with a mournful beat. "Just A Closer Walk With Thee" was a must. No doubt, some of the onlookers heard it and smiled as they thought of the other version:

Just a bowl of butterbeans;
Pass the cornbread if you please.
I don't want no turnip greens;
All I want is a bowl of butterbeans.

This quaint New Orleans funeral tradition gave rise to a whole genre of music called "Tailgate Jazz."

New Orleans has changed a lot since the days when funeral processions featured horse-drawn wagons. I wonder if New Orleanians stop for processions these days? Are there any old jazzmen left to play "Just A Closer Walk?"

Why this tradition of stopping for a funeral procession? Perhaps it's just a gesture of respect for the departed and their bereaved. But maybe it's more than that. Maybe it's part of the shared Southern experience that puts so much stock in the continuum of existence: birth and death, seedtime and harvest, family and friends, the special ties of time and place.

Then too, maybe there's something about the cherished notion that life in the South for much of the past century and a half has been a struggle. We struggle into this life and we struggle out. And it's nice to know that as we make our exit, folks are kind and considerate enough to just be quiet for a moment.

Seasons of the Heart

The Guitar Man and the Lady from Frisco

They are a vanload of pilgrims, climbing through the swirling snow of a late December night from the Denver airport up toward ski country — a family from Missouri, another from North Carolina, a couple of college kids headed home for the holidays. And the Guitar Man.

He wears jeans and a faded leather jacket. His luggage consists of a duffel bag and a battered guitar case — a six-stringed Martin or Gibson, probably, wood worn bare by the brushing wings of a million notes and chords. He's in his late twenties and he has a nice smile. But he has a road-weary look about him, sort of like his guitar case.

The van driver is a jolly sort who keeps up a running conversation with his passengers — partly to relieve the boredom of the trip he makes up and down I-70 so many times that every boulder, every snow-crusted pine is etched in his subconscious; but also because he's genuinely interested in people and he's full of the holiday spirit. He's got Arthur Fiedler and the Boston Pops playing "Good King Wenceslas" on the stereo. And he wants to know who the pilgrims are and where they're from. That's how they get to know that they're Missourians and Carolinians and college students, trading names and places and bits of personal background here in the warm temporary intimacy of a rubber-tired cocoon.

The last to speak is the Guitar Man, who says he's a folksinger. He's been traveling the East, playing coffee houses and college campuses and small bars, trying to figure out if he can make a living with his music. He's soft-spoken and engagingly modest and the rest of the passengers can hear the music in his voice — a traveling troubadour, a man who tells stories in song. And he has a story of his own.

There's a Lady in Frisco, a little mountain town just off the interstate. A rather special lady, or at least she used to be. She and the Guitar Man were more than friends once upon a time not too long ago, until the music took hold and pulled him out on the road. The Lady in Frisco begged him not to go. But it was something he just had to do. The music was strong inside him — stronger, he thought, than love. So he went, hoping that maybe love would wait. During these long months while he was out there in the coffee houses and bars, the Guitar Man and the Lady in Frisco haven't spoken or written, not once. That was the way she wanted it.

Now, on this snowy night just before Christmas, the Guitar Man is headed back to Frisco, back to the tiny apartment where the Lady lives, carrying his duffel bag and his guitar and his heart. The Lady in Frisco doesn't know he's coming. And he doesn't know what he'll find when he gets there. Maybe there's someone else. Maybe she's so hurt and disappointed, maybe she thinks he's so unreliable, she doesn't want to see him any more. She may not let him in. But he's come all this way to try.

The Guitar Man's fellow pilgrims are all but

struck dumb by his bittersweet story and by the anticipation of what's to come. The Guitar Man will be the first passenger to disembark, and all of the others will get to see if the Lady in Frisco turns him away. If she does, he'll ride on to the next town and find a place to crash for the night.

The van climbs on, past the meadow where the buffalo herd hunkers against the frigid night, past the rocks where the big-horn sheep scramble by day, up and over the Continental Divide. The driver and the pilgrims are quiet, lost in their thoughts, considering the Continental Divide of the heart where east meets west and sometimes the altitude and the bitter wind are too much, where even the most resolute traveler has to turn back and seek shelter elsewhere.

On the stereo, the joyous strings of the Boston Pops ring out, "Oh Come All Ye Faithful." But the pilgrims hear another song of another season:

> *Rambling man, why don't you settle down;*
> *Boston ain't your kind of town;*
> *There ain't no gold*
> *and there ain't nobody like me.*

And then they're in Frisco and the van is crunching along a back street, pulling up in front of a row of one-story apartments. Inside the van, you can hear a pin drop. The Guitar Man climbs out. "Good luck," the driver says. The Guitar Man smiles, then closes the door behind him, hoists his duffel bag and guitar case, and climbs the steps. There's a Christmas tree in the window, all decorated with colored lights and tinsel. But for the pilgrims in the van, their faces pressed to the windows, it won't be Christmas unless....

The Guitar Man knocks. The door opens, the rectangle of light framing a young woman in a bathrobe. The folks in the van can't see her face very well, but they can imagine surprise, shock, maybe even anger. Or maybe nothing. That would be the worst. "Come on lady," somebody in the van says softly, "let him in." But they stand there in the light for a long moment, the Guitar Man and the Lady from Frisco, oblivious to the cold, the rest of their lives hanging in the balance.

Then she steps back from the door, making room for him. The Guitar Man turns and gives the van folk a thumb's up and then he enters and closes the door behind him. In the van, they're cheering and crying.

The pilgrims move on into the night, now lovely and silent and at peace with itself, all of them touched in some deep place of the soul they had forgotten was there.

Serendipity in the Spring Garden

When Spring arrives, remember: it's time for sterile poo-poo.

My late father-in-law, Paul Strong of Birmingham, introduced me to sterile poo-poo many years ago. It's one of the things about him I treasure because it said so much about the quality of the man.

It all started when the City of Birmingham began marketing treated sewage sludge. Some enterprising official at the waste treatment plant thought it was a way to turn a by-product into profit for the city coffers. So local gardening shops started selling sewage sludge by the bag, and Papa Strong zeroed in on it like a homing pigeon. He was a dedicated and enthusiastic gardener, but more than that, he liked nothing better than a new idea.

As I remember, the early sales of what he called "sterile poo-poo" were sluggish. The city assured everyone that it was completely safe and sanitary, but Birmingham folks were slow to cotton to the idea of strewing sewage around their lawns, flower beds and vegetable gardens. Papa Strong was undaunted. He toted home several bags from K-Mart and began to work it into the already-rich soil of his planting beds. It worked passably well on such things as azaleas and nandina bushes. But where it really shone was with the elephant ears.

You're familiar with elephant ears — a tuberous plant that dies back to nothing in the winter, but begins to sprout shoots at the first hint of warm weather. Soon, you have long, thin stalks with big leaves at the end — in the shape of, well, elephant ears.

In most cases, elephant ears reach about waist high at full growth. But not with Papa Strong. He fed his plant a steady diet of sterile poo-poo through the Spring growing season, and by midsummer he had a phenomenon on his hands. His elephant ears shaded the patio. The stalks were a good eight feet long, and the leaves were three feet from end to end. Papa Strong's flower bed looked like a tropical rain forest. We expected natives to appear at any moment.

The elephant ears became a source of wonder and awe. Sales of treated sewage sludge began to soar as the word got out about what was happening in Papa Strong's back yard. Folks would come from miles around to gawk in amazement.

"How do you do it?" the gawkers would ask.

Papa Strong would smile and say, "Sterile poo-poo."

He should have gotten a cut of the profits from the city, or at least a civic service award. "Man of the Year" wouldn't have been excessive. But Papa Strong was never much for awards. His satisfaction was in trying something new. He was, throughout his long life, an innovator, a thinker, a discoverer — always open to a new way of doing things. He delighted in experimentation, and thus he was always being charmed by serendipity. And he was the kind of guy who could say "sterile poo-poo" and make it sound like a French eau-de-cologne.

At age 67, Paul Strong was struck by a devastating stroke. He lay in a coma for days, and his doctors gave him up for dead on a daily basis. But every morning when the sun came up, he was still hanging grimly to life. Eventually, he regained consciousness and went home — partially paralyzed and much reduced physically, but with his mind and spirit quite intact.

Papa Strong lived for seventeen more years, nurtured by the gentle, loving care of his devoted wife Lillian and his four children. I never heard him utter a breath of complaint. And I never knew him to lose his sense of humor or his sense of wonder at the possibilities in life. He awoke every morning with the idea that he would be better by the time he went to sleep that night, and he worked hard all day to realize his goal. He exercised his stroke-damaged limbs and his mind. He read voraciously, relished surprise, enjoyed travel and lively conversation, and above all continued to be open to the magic of new ideas. Serendipity followed him through his life like a guardian angel because he fertilized his soul with the spiritual equivalent of sterile poo-poo.

Every spring, my thoughts are enriched with the memory of Paul Strong. He was my hero, one of the finest men I have ever had the privilege to know, and I count myself fortunate for having spent some time with him. There was a marvelous childlike quality about him — a wide-eyed, wondrous combination of spunk and imagination. Like his elephant ears, he never stopped growing. He was a man of sterile poo-poo. I should be half so lucky.

The Peace of Wild Things

I floated down the New River on my inner tube and came into the peace of wild things.

The phrase comes from a Wendell Berry poem:

When despair for the world grows in me...
I go and lie down where the wood drake rests
in his beauty on the water,
and the great heron feeds.
I come into the peace of wild things....

I can't say that despair for the world had grown in me, because by nature I'm not the despairing type. But it had been an especially hectic day — noisy and demanding. So late in the afternoon, I turned from the world and headed for the river with my inner tube. By the time I emerged from the water two hours later, the wild things had restored my sense of balance and beauty.

The New River is born in North Carolina's Watauga County and flows north into Virginia. It eventually becomes quite impressive, especially as it thunders through West Virginia's New River Gorge. But the stretch I love is not many miles from its headwaters where it is a modest, shallow stream with an occasional murmuring rapid. There are long stretches where you see no sign of habitation, only the gray-green of water dappled by sun and shadow, thickets of rhododendron nestled among the oaks and maples and locusts that grow close to the banks, the soft colors of wildflowers — bee's balm, Queen Anne's lace, ladyslipper — and creatures that swim and slither and crawl and fly.

There is, on special occasions, a great heron that feeds at the water's edge, stepping delicately about on stilted legs. If you are very quiet and still, he will let the river carry you past without taking flight. There are also rare glimpses of a family of wood ducks or a solitary water snake rippling across the surface. On this day, the heron and the ducks and the snake have business elsewhere. So I content myself for awhile with the common birds — a splash of Cardinal red, a mottled brown thrush, a goldfinch in spectacular dipping flight.

And then, not far from journey's end, serendipity. I detect a tiny movement on the water's surface to my right and turn slowly and carefully to see a small brown head bobbing along — a muskrat. Another, a female, waits on a nearby log. He climbs up beside her and they both eye me for a moment. Then she slips into the water and disappears toward a pile of twigs and brush along the bank: home. He continues to sit, taking the late afternoon air, paying me scant attention as I disappear around a bend in the river. It is tempting to give them a human story — Mrs. Musk-rat welcoming Mr. at the end of a busy day. But the charm of wild things is that they are *not* human. So I let muskrats be muskrats.

And then, a few minutes later, a great rustle of wings at the top of a buckeye tree to my left. I catch just a glimpse of the eagle as he takes flight, heading up and away behind the trees toward the ridge line where he lives. It is a heart-stopping moment. I've heard tales about him, but this is my first sighting. It may be a great while before there is another. He is a shy and wily creature.

I am fortunate to have the river to myself this late afternoon. There are no canoe-loads of noisy tourists, talking nonstop and banging their paddles against the sides of their canoes. They miss a great deal. To really *see* the river, to truly enter the realm of the wild things, you have to be still and quiet. There is a temptation on an innertube to flail the water and try to direct your progress, like the canoeists do. But you eventually learn that if you simply drift, the river will bear you unerringly along. And as you drift, you will be rewarded. Your soul, by journey's end, will be rested.

Much of the world is a noisy, clamoring affair, and we sacrifice our sense of what is worthwhile if we don't find a way to escape to a place where we can listen to the secrets of our own hearts. You can find such a place by turning off the TV and closing the door. But to experience the special peace of wild things, you have to go into their places — a back yard in early morning, a secluded corner of a park, woods or field, the river at late afternoon.

If you do, you will know of what Wendell Berry felt and wrote:

For a time I rest in the grace of the world and am free.

A Vow, A Kiss, and Off They Go Together

I t was 9:30 on a Friday morning when Billy and Alison showed up at the magistrate's office. They had already been over to the courthouse and they had the necessary paperwork, and now they wanted to get married.

What you need to get married in the state of North Carolina is a man and a woman, a license, a duly sworn officer of the law to perform the nuptials, two witnesses, and ten bucks. There was a highway patrolman shooting the breeze in the magistrate's office and this other fellow standing out in the hallway. "You wouldn't want to be a witness at a wedding, would you?" Billy tentatively asked the other fellow.

"Sure," the other fellow said. "I've been married more than thirty years, and maybe my being a witness will bring you good luck."

So with the highway patrolman and this other fellow lined up to witness, Billy and Alison stood before the magistrate's desk. They looked to be in their late teens or early '20s. Billy had long hair and a brave attempt at a beard. Alison was a pretty young thing, wearing an ankle-length tie-dyed dress and a shy smile. They both looked a little scared, but very much in love. You could see it in their eyes and the way they held onto each other. Entering into marriage probably should be a little scary, because it's pretty serious business. But if you're enough in love, you'll over-come the fright and take the plunge.

"Do you have rings?" the magistrate asked.

Well no, Billy and Alison didn't have rings. They were exchanging their hearts, and that seemed to be enough. The magistrate smiled. "Well, we'll just dispense with the ring part of the ceremony."

The magistrate pulled a piece of paper out of his drawer. The vows. The witnesses could tell the magistrate had performed this ceremony many times in his career, but he seemed to be the kind of fellow who never took it for granted. Probably has a pretty good marriage himself and remem-bers what it's like to start out young and in love and without much in the way of worldly goods. So the magistrate summoned his best magisterial manner and gave the ceremony the gravity and solemnity it deserved.

It's pretty simple stuff, this marrying — at least the formal, legal part. "I, Billy, take thee Alison..." and vice-versa. To have and to hold, in sickness and health, in good times and bad, when supper's on time and when it's not, when you pick up your dirty underwear and when you don't, until death us do part. It was over in a matter of min-utes and then the magistrate pronounced them man and wife and Billy kissed the bride. It was a beautiful kiss, and everybody in the room was just a trifle misty-eyed, even the straight-arrow young highway patrolman.

"That'll be ten dollars," the magistrate said.

Billy and Alison looked stricken. Billy fished in his pocket and pulled out a thin crumple of bills. A five, a couple of ones.

Alison reached for her pocketbook. "Can you take a personal check?"

"Sorry," the magistrate said. "No personal checks. It's a state rule."

Barely married, and already a financial crisis. Not the last, to be sure. *("You spent the last thirty dollars on WHAT?")* But this was no time for a spoiler. This other fellow pulled out his billfold, gave the magistrate a ten-dollar bill and said, "It's on me." The highway patrolman then said, "Your first wedding present!" The smiles on Billy's and Alison's faces said it was as good a present as they could imagine. Of course, with a gift comes advice. "Cling to each other," this other fellow said. "And give a little."

This fellow says whenever he goes to a wedding, he remembers the advice from the minister who married him and his wife more than thirty years ago. "It's not enough for you to meet each other halfway," the minister told the young couple. "Each of you has to be able to go all the way, to make one hundred percent of the effort to patch up a disagreement. If you're both willing to give one hundred percent, you'll overlap in the middle and everything will work out."

Billy and Alison solemnly promised to heed the fellow's advice, and then they went out into the morning, married folks by 9:45 with the rest of the day and a lifetime ahead of them. And the magistrate and the highway patrolman and this other fellow went back to doing whatever it is they do when they're not marrying folks or witnessing.

But this other fellow says it was the best thing that's happened to him in a long time. He went home and hugged his wife and told her how much he loves her and how glad he is they overcame their fright and struck out together more than thirty years ago. Since that experience, he has felt himself in a certain state of grace. He's even made an extra effort to pick up his dirty underwear.

This fellow doubts he'll ever see Billy and Alison again. They've disappeared into the mass of humanity who try to get by day-to-day, celebrate joys, handle sorrows, brave the cold winds and keep faith with their own and each other's hearts. He hopes they make it. All he had to contribute was ten bucks and his blessing. Maybe that helps a little.

Santa's Coming Regardless

Every year when Christmas approaches, the anxiety level reaches nuclear proportions. And I don't mean parents, either. It's the kids who are truly worried, and grown-ups are the reason. The air is full of dire threats about what might happen to that eagerly anticipated visit from Santa if children aren't something close to saintly.

Grown-ups have been putting the evil eye

on children's behavior since time immemorial. Imagine a cave-dwelling mother: "If you don't eat your supper, a saber tooth tiger will eat you."

My grandmother had a special word of terror for young folks who trampled her flowers, tracked mud on her rug, or swung too high in her porch swing. "Nasty stinkin' young'uns," she'd bark, "I'm gonna pinch your heads off." Mama Cooper was a sweet and kind person who never would have pinched the head off a radish, much less a child, but she could strike fear into her grandchildren. We were careful around her flowers, her rug and her porch swing.

So scaring young folks is a time-honored tradition. But the direst predictions of ruin and misfortune, it seems, are always saved for the Christmas season. "If you don't clean your plate, Santa Claus won't come." "Act ugly one more time, buster, and you'll find a bag of switches under the tree for you on Christmas morning." Well, baloney.

I came to my senses about the Santa Claus business when I met Jake Tibbetts, a crotchety old newspaper editor who appeared in my imagination one day and then took over the pages of my first novel, *Home Fires Burning.* Jake had a built-in bull-hockey detector, and he could spot nonsense a mile away. Jake's grandson Lonnie lived with Jake and his wife Pastine, and when Christmas rolled around, Mama Pastine put the pox on Lonnie about Santa's upcoming visit.

At the breakfast table one morning, Lonnie let a mild oath slip from his ten-year-old lips. "Santa Claus has no truck with blasphemers," Mama Pastine said.

"Hogwash," Daddy Jake snorted. "Santa Claus makes no moral judgments. His sole responsibility is to make young folks happy. Even bad ones. Even TERRIBLE ones."

"Then why," Lonnie asked, "does he bring switches to some kids?"

Jake replied, "This business about switches is pure folklore. Did you ever know anybody who really got switches for Christmas? Even one?"

Lonnie couldn't think of a single one.

"Right," said Daddy Jake. "I have been on this earth for sixty-four years, and I have encountered some of the meanest, vilest, smelliest, most undeserving creatures the Good Lord ever allowed to creep and crawl. And not one of them ever got switches for Christmas. Lots of 'em were *told* they'd get switches. Lots of 'em laid in their beds trembling through Christmas Eve, just knowing they'd find a stocking full of hickory branches come morning. But you know what they found? Goodies. Even the worst of 'em got some kind of goodies. And for one small instant, every child who lives and breathes is happy and good, even if he is as mean as a snake every other instant. That's what Santa Claus is for, anyhow."

Well, Daddy Jake said it better than I ever could. I believe with all my heart that he is right, just as I believe fervently in Santa Claus and always have.

I believed in Santa Claus even through the Great Fort Bragg Misbehavior of 1953. My father was stationed at Fort Bragg with the Army, and I was in the fourth grade at the post elementary school. The day before school let out for the Christmas holidays, Santa Claus landed on the playground in an Army helicopter. It was, to me and my classmates, something akin to the Second Coming. When we went out to welcome Santa, the teachers stationed the first-through-fourth graders on one side of the playground and the fifth and sixth graders on the other. When Santa's chopper landed, I learned why. We little kids were yelling our heads off for Santa to leave us some goodies under the tree a few nights hence. Across the way, the fifth and sixth graders were yelling, "Fake! Fake!" Some of my classmates were crestfallen. It never fazed me. I figured those big kids were wrong then, and still do. Santa Claus is for real. Just look in a kid's eyes and you'll see him. (By the way, I'm sure the fifth and sixth graders didn't get switches for Christmas. Maybe they should have, but they didn't.)

Grown-ups are wrong, too, when they threaten kids with the loss of Santa. Daddy Jake was right. We adult types need to grant the kids their unfettered moment of magic. If they act up, threaten to pinch their heads off. But leave Santa out of it.

The Unending Journey of the Footsore Pilgrim

I'm told that Henry Waterson, the long-time editor of the Louisville *Courier-Journal,* kept a sign on his desk that read, "LORD, GIVE ME THIS DAY MY DAILY IDEA. AND FORGIVE ME THE ONE I HAD YESTERDAY."

It's a good motto for a journalist, and it says a lot about why bright, energetic, creative people stay in a business where the pay is low, the hours are bad, and the customers are often disgruntled. What keeps a good journalist coming back is the idea that every day, you start fresh with a new set of events, a new cast of characters, an odd twist or turn of the human comedy. A journalist who is truly hooked on the business delights in surprise, in discovery, and in the process of searching: for fact, for opinion, for hidden agenda. In short, for understanding.

But this isn't about journalism. It's about that broader idea of searching, of seeking, that involves all of us. It's about what I've come to believe is both the great joy and great pain of being human. The hunger to know. The agony of realizing we can't know everything. The ongoing battle inside us between faith and reason.

My favorite writer is the late Walker Percy — born in Birmingham, raised in Mississippi, educated at Chapel Hill. Percy became a physician, but early in his professional life he contracted tuberculosis. He was forced into exile in a sanitorium where he began to read and ask questions. Later, when he was cured and settled in Louisiana, he began to write about his questions — or, more accurately, his quest. His first novel, *The Moviegoer,* won the National Book Award. He went on to write other works of fiction and philosophy that are both hugely entertaining and disturbingly profound. Had he not died of cancer several years ago, I feel sure he would have won a Nobel Prize for literature.

Percy wrote of man as a "sovereign wayfarer." He said that God has placed us in the cosmic pecking order above the beasts, but below the angels. And he said we are doomed to wander like footsore pilgrims in the great gulf between angel and beast, trying to figure out who in the heck we really are. Along the way, we find elements of both angel and beast in our character. But we never get a precise handle on our nature. That's okay, Percy thought, because the quest for identity is the great human endeavor, the agony and ecstasy of being alive.

It's a state of affairs against which we often rebel. This is a complex, fast-moving, perilous and confusing world we live in. The traffic is bad, the kid has an ear-ache, the boss is unreasonable, the paycheck won't quite stretch to fit the lifestyle, and all our heroes have clay feet. Sooner or later, we cry out to the world, "I'm fed up and I'm not gonna take it any more. I want some *answers,* by God." Then along comes somebody with what appears to be a simple formula that explains everything. And we're tempted to embrace it with blind, fanatical zeal. An easy answer is a safe, warm cocoon in which we can take refuge from the world.

Walker Percy wouldn't buy that. Lower forms of life might be content with following rigid patterns that are bred into their gene pool by centuries of evolution, but human beings are better than that. We can't understand perfectly, the way angels can, but we can reason. We can question. We can search. He believed that if we surrender our reason to ideologies or institutions or causes or particular people, we violate our basic nature. He didn't mean we shouldn't support a cause or embrace a belief. But he thought we should know *why.* And that requires a quest.

I think today's young people have by and large got it right. When my generation went out into the world as young adults, we were driven by a desire to settle into a career, find the right mate, surround ourselves with the right things. Many of us have arrived at mid-life divorced, downsized, and disillusioned. Today's young — the ones I talk with — seem much more open to possibilities, much more honest with themselves about the potential joys and pitfalls they face. They, too, may end up divorced and downsized. But I don't believe they'll be quite as disillusioned. They don't have a lot of illusions going in, and they appear fairly comfortable with the fluid, complex world they are entering. They seem to embrace life as a quest. Walker Percy would be proud.

Percy — a Catholic — would also be heartened by the encyclical published by Pope John Paul. It's called "Faith and Reason" and it embraces the notion of this duality of man's quest. Faith is strongest when it is attained by asking the tough questions, seeking honest answers, arriving at an understanding of why we believe. And being open to change.

The Pope may have read Walker Percy. And he might have enjoyed Henry Waterson. "Lord, give me this day my daily idea...."

Memories from the Edge of the World

To the beach for a weekend wedding, the handsome son of friends marrying a lovely young lady to whom he has been paying court for ten years, since they met in college. There's something to be said for taking your time getting into a business as serious as marriage. I would offer it as advice, except for the fact that I didn't follow it myself. Paulette and I first laid eyes on each other on the weekend after Thanksgiving in 1966, and the following April 15th, we were wed. Roughly four and a half months to decide that we couldn't do without each other, send out invitations, and tie the knot. A risky notion, probably. That was more than thirty years ago.

The Litchfield wedding was our first time at the beach in years. It used to be a yearly summer ritual, a week at places along the Gulf, Panama City and Gulf Shores, and up and down the coast of the Carolinas: Sunset, Edisto, Hilton Head, Emerald Isle. Long walks, thick books, the company of good friends, kids splashing at water's edge, sand castles, crab gumbo. Children becoming teenagers and then moving on into worlds of their own. The scrapbooks of our memories are filled with scenes and anecdotes, the "do you remember..." that adds texture to our older lives.

But for the past ten years or so, we've spent our spare time in the mountains, joined often in the warm months by family and friends for tubing on the river, backyard cookouts, day trips to flea markets and country stores and barbecue havens. New scrapbooks are filling now with people and experiences. Some of the people exist only in the memory of their visit and the indelible imprint they left on our lives. They have passed on, but they haven't truly left us.

The mountains shelter us a way the beach never did. The beach is yawning space, limitless sky and sea. The mountains seem to hover, always rising a bit above wherever you stand. And when the fog rolls in off the river, it envelops everything in a close grayness that invites you to stay inside and build a fire, even in the summer, and brew a pot of tea and think on those things Faulkner spoke of as "the secrets of the human heart."

The beach, at least the part we visited on the wedding weekend, has changed profoundly since we were there ten years ago. And yet, in a special way, it hasn't. If you stand at mid-beach and look to the land, you see an almost solid wall of high rises, club houses, elegant homes, cell phone towers. But if you turn and look in the other direction, you can forget for a moment that the man-made structures are there. You see sand and wave, ever-changing sky and sun-speckled Atlantic meeting at a horizon that is achingly far. Children splash at water's edge and grow before your eyes into gangly teenagers taking their first tentative steps into the daunting, intriguing "out there."

Low tide. A gaggle of kids, most of them elementary age, burrow like moles in the sand, constructing an elaborate maze of trenches, castles and bunkers. They have dug down to that magical sea-level place where water rises unbidden in the bottom of your hole, and no matter how much you scoop and bail with your plastic bucket or shovel, the water keeps flooding in and collapsing the sides of your sand pit. The runny sand you get from the bottom of your child-made tidal pool drips through small fingers and makes delicate gray stalagmites to adorn the parapets of the sand castle you are constructing — a home for the beautiful Princess Kay and the jolly fire-breathing dragon who lives in the dungeon and who emerges at dusk to light the royal barbecue grill.

Up and down the beach, the children are an

army of construction workers worthy of the Grand Coulee Dam or the Panama Canal, each project a fertile garden patch where the imagination grows. There was nothing here but sand, and now it is being transformed into hundreds of tiny worlds where anything is possible.

To the grown-up walking the beach at low tide, there's an element, I suppose, of bitter-sweetness here. You realize that tides are inexorable and inevitable, and that soon, all this carefully-built children's world will be covered by water. Hours later, when the ocean retreats again, there will not be so much as a trace of all that labor, all that fantasy. It gives the grown-up a sharp sense of the impermanence of any imprint man seeks to put upon the earth — the impermanence, more acutely, of man himself. And if you stand on the beach long enough and look out to sea and let the vastness of it take hold, you get the sense of existing at the very edge of the world, in a spot that is exhilaratingly precarious. Only a tentative thing called gravity holds you here. You could, but for a slender thread of physics, fly away. And someday, you will.

But children don't dwell upon such things. A beach swept clean by tide is simply a place to begin, a slate wiped clean, an invitation. A place to begin storing away memories that will be pleasant company by the fires of later years when the fog rolls in.

Comets, Cotton and History

Remember Hale-Bopp? What a marvelous comet it was back in 1997, making a vivid splash across the northwest sky just at Easter, which we think of as a time of wonder and discovery.

Hale-Bopp wasn't discovered until July, 1995, when two astronomers — a professional and an amateur, working separately — spotted it. But using the tools of physics and mathematics, scientists have learned that Hale-Bopp has been around for a long time. The last time it passed by earth, they say, was 4,200 years ago.

My wife, Paulette, observed that if there were intelligent creatures looking down on earth from Hale-Bopp, they'd be saying, "Gee, that place has changed a lot since we were last in the neighborhood."

When the comet sped by in 2213 B.C., the pyramids of Egypt were new and the great civilizations of Greece and Rome were far in the future. Mankind was beginning to show glimmers of the creative thought that would form our modern world. Europeans were tilling the land with plows and the Chinese had invented irrigation and metalworking. But much of the natural world was shrouded in myth and magic. The Chinese, for example, explained an eclipse of the sun by saying a dragon had eaten it. Their version is a great deal more fun than the modern one.

As Paulette and I were watching Hale-Bopp, I started thinking about Price McLemore.

When I knew him thirty years ago, Price McLemore was a cotton farmer near Montgomery, Alabama. He loved the feel of the soil, the rhythms of the seasons, and the notion that the land he farmed was tied by blood and sweat to the history of his family.

One spring day, in the little outbuilding he called an office, he showed me his journal — a big leather-bound ledger that was a chronicle of the McLemore farm. It went back more than a hundred years to the time before the Civil War. Every McLemore who had farmed the land had made an entry in the journal every day of the cotton-growing season every year. They started at planting time and went through harvest. It was a matter of honor that no McLemore ever missed an entry.

Each recorded faithfully what the weather was like on a particular day, how the crop was progressing, the rainfall, battles against boll weevils. Over time, the McLemores discovered that seasons repeated themselves. No matter what the present year was like, you could probably find a year somewhere in the past that resembled it. And that could help you plan on how to spray and fertilize and when to hire workers to help harvest the crop.

It may have been a crude kind of science, but it worked for the McLemores. And for me, it reinforced the notion that man and nature are one — each with its seasons, repeating themselves in universal timelessness. Birth and death, seedtime and harvest. What goes around, comes around — like crops and comets. There's a comfort and a hopefulness in that.

We are often quick to toss off our past — or worse, to ignore it. We devastate rain forests and bulldoze buildings. We rewrite history in the name of political correctness. And we consign reams of classic literature to the trash heap simply because it was written by dead guys. We want everything to be new and shiny, and we try to tell ourselves that everything that's worthwhile, we invented yesterday. Our children don't know who wrote the Declaration of Independence, much less who were the first humans to employ the plow in agriculture.

But I think we're fooling ourselves. There is nothing truly new under the sun, only what was already there, waiting to be found.

We humans are smart and clever, but often we lack wisdom — a virtue that is cultivated in part through an appreciation of the past. As one perceptive fellow put it, we rarely see the handwriting on the wall until our backs are to it. We can find the handwriting in the form of hieroglyphs and primitive paintings on cave walls. It is in bound leather journals that record the ebb and flow of a cotton farm's seasons of life. It appears as a bright smudge in the northwest sky on a clear March evening.

Perhaps when we consider Hale-Bopp or other heavenly bodies, it can be a catalyst for rediscovering the charm and usefulness of history. We can see a comet not as a bright smudge, but as a visitor from the distant past. We can watch it with a sense of myth and magic, awe and wonder, and say, "Oh, how far we have come. And how incredibly far we have to go."

Considering Life Without Pluto

My seatmate on the flight to Fort Myers is, I'm guessing, about 75 — petite, white-haired, lively of eye and pleasant of manner. She's dressed comfortably for travel in slacks and cotton blouse, and in the overhead bin she has stowed away a nice, warm coat because she has come down from Connecticut just this morning. They've had lots of ice and snow in Connecticut during the winter, but all that is behind her now.

She's on her way to Fort Myers, she tells me, for a little vacation. Actually, her destination is Naples, a few miles south of Fort Myers. It's a tradition she's observed for a dozen years — a month of Florida warmth while Connecticut skids and shivers. She has five friends who are year-round residents of Naples, and they'll be waiting for her at the Fort Myers airport.

There's one thing different about the trip this year. It's the first time she's made it alone. She buried her husband a month ago. I say the usual awkward sympathies and watch the little etchings of pain around her eyes. But she's handling it well. The friends in Naples are a big help. They've told her, "You'll never be homeless." I realize that means a lot more than just a place of physical shelter, especially now. So she will spend a few days with each of her Naples friends and then fly back to Connecticut, knowing that it's not her only home.

She's doing okay, I think. I hope that one day, if faced with similar circumstances, I could handle such a loss with as much grace and that I would have five friends somewhere who would make sure I'm never homeless.

Still, despite grace and friends, I can sense the immensity of my seatmate's loss. I'm sitting now where her husband sat all those years. I can be a companionable fellow traveler for an hour and a half, but I don't nearly fill the seat.

I've brought a newspaper along, and I offer to share it, but my seatmate's vision is deteriorating and she needs a special device to read. It's an aggravation that she copes with, but she can't share my newspaper. So as I read about the vast world, she's quietly lost in private thought, perhaps thinking of a snow-covered grave in Connecticut — and, hopefully, of those friends waiting at the Fort Myers airport.

There's a story in the paper about Pluto, my favorite planet. I've always liked Pluto because it has a neat name, one that Walt Disney appropriated for the lovable cartoon dog. This newspaper story says Pluto (the planet, not the dog) is in danger of being downsized. Pluto is both the smallest planet and the one farthest from the sun — a tiny orb out there on the fringe of our solar system. And now, some astronomers are of the opinion that it doesn't qualify as a planet at all, not in the sense of the eight others that include our relatively-puny earth and such giants as Jupiter and Saturn. These scientists want to reclassify Pluto as a "minor planet," or worse, lump it into an undignified class of heavenly "ice balls." In either case, we would no longer call it Pluto. We would give it a number. How cruel.

Across the aisle is a man about the same age as my seatmate. The woman sitting next to him appears to be his wife. He's impatient with her, out of sorts in a sour, scrunched-faced way. When she has to get up to go to the bathroom, he makes a bit of a show of being discommoded. After she returns, he has two Bloody Marys and drifts off to sleep, snoring. His wife seems relieved. I wish I could introduce her to my seatmate and that they could steal away together, leaving the impatient, snoring husband behind, head down to Naples for a month of fun in the sun, good seafood, shopping, a walk on the beach. One's loss might be tempered by the other's freedom.

But of course the wife would never do such a thing. Somehow she's put up with grumpiness all these years and here in the twilight she's not likely to exchange the known for the unknown. They wear each other, I suspect, like old shoes — one simply more tattered and ill-fitting than the other. I think of Jimmy Dean, the country singer and sausage-maker, who said, "Dance with the one that brung ya." Maybe she will just keep dancing, but occasionally kick him in the shins until his disposition improves. Someday, odds are, she will lose him. And she will miss him, grumpiness and all.

I read the story about Pluto again and ponder for awhile on the nature of loss and its aftermath. If the scientists get their way, if Pluto gets downsized to minor planet or ice ball, I'll never again think of the solar system in quite the same way.

Maybe the other planets — especially the ones nearest Pluto, will take him in and vow that he will never be homeless. Still, I'll miss Pluto. You don't replace a planet. Or a person. Friends help, life goes on. But it's not ever quite the same.

Christmas Is Worth
a Tear or Two

As TV-radio host Art Linkletter used to say, "Kids say the darndest things." Sometimes what they say has such innocent clarity that it becomes pure wisdom.

I thought about that when a friend shared with me some quotes from children — the kinds of things that grown-ups overhear and pass along. One sixth grade girl said, "I like my teacher because she always cries when we sing 'Silent Night.'"

Do you cry when you sing or hear "Silent Night?" I do, unashamedly. I'm not sure I can put my finger on exactly why. I suppose it's partly the lovely, simple words and melody. I don't get the same feeling about "Good King Wenceslas," which has a sort of rousing good cheer to it. "Silent Night" is sung slowly, with feeling, best done in a dim sanctuary with a lighted candle in hand. There is something about the song that evokes all of the bittersweetness of the holiday season — of joy and sorrow, of things present and things past, of people cherished and people mourned.

I remember the first time I ever cried over "Silent Night." I was a teenager, a member of the Methodist Youth Fellowship in my little South Alabama hometown. On the Sunday night before Christmas, it was tradition for the church youth to forego our usual meeting and instead go caroling about the community. Some of us could sing and some couldn't, but we all made a joyful noise of one kind or another, and when we finished our rounds and went back to the church for brownies and hot chocolate, we were richly warmed with the spirit of the season. I remember that we were unusually subdued on those occasions, our teen-aged souls touched by something deeper than the mere singing of songs.

We caroled mostly for the benefit of the town's sick and shut-in. And in a town of 4,000, we included just about anybody who had the least kind of malady, from terminal illness to ingrown toenail, so there would be enough recipients to make it a worthwhile evening.

This one Christmas I remember so vividly, my grandmother, my beloved Mama Cooper, was on our caroling list. She had been down with a cold and had not been able to attend services at the Methodist Church that weekend. So the Youth Fellowship showed up on her doorstep on Sunday night about eight. She bundled herself in scarf and overcoat and stood in her open doorway while we sang a carol. And then she requested "Silent Night."

As we began to sing, I looked into Mama Cooper's aging face and confronted, for the very first time, her mortality. Mama Cooper was a pow-erfully sweet influence on my young life — men-tor, cheerleader, protector, confidant, friend — all those things only a grandmother can be. I was the oldest grandchild and occupied a special place in her small universe. I suppose I had assumed she would always be there. But in that instant I realized that she wouldn't, and I was devastated. So I stood there on the back row with tears rolling down my cheeks, my voice caught in my throat, and — purely and simply — grieved.

Mama Cooper lived for another 30 years or so, and I had the continued blessing of her com-panionship right up to the end. I think I always appreciated her a little more after that December

Sunday night on her front porch when I was a mere, half-formed lad. At her funeral, when her other grandsons and I bore her to her gravesite, I silently sang "Silent Night." And I cried — not so much because she was gone, but because of what she had left in my heart.

I have a good friend who lost his wife a couple of years ago. They were a devoted couple. He still misses her terribly and always will. He tells the story of being in Marine Corps boot camp during World War Two, when the drill sergeant brought word to one of the recruits that his mother had passed away. The recruit started crying and the drill sergeant dressed him down. "Marines don't cry," the sergeant said. But my friend says the sergeant was wrong. There are some things worth crying over, even for Marines.

I think it's perfectly okay to cry. Some guys think not and make a superhuman effort not to. But I believe allowing yourself to cry is an act of courage — admitting that you have the capacity to be deeply affected by something or someone, to be vulnerable to the whole range of human emotion.

Tears are worth shedding for all sorts of reasons, many of them perfectly happy ones. And the holiday season is a perfectly good time to do so. We cry because of the people we miss, and we shed tears of joy for those we cling to. We cry over precious memories and over the gift of the days to come when we can say the things we need to say, do the things we need to do, for those who are still with us.

I try to take a moment during the week before each Christmas, right by myself, to light a candle in a darkened room and sing "Silent Night." I launch out bravely, but there's no way I get all the way through it. No matter. It's a special thing to take into the new year.

The Graduation Speech I Should Have Given

I've heard a lot of graduation speeches over the years and given a few of them myself. They're mostly full of high-sounding and entirely worthy ideas, meant to inspire the graduates to lives of diligence, integrity and commitment. We need speeches like that to remind us of the loftiest goals in life, of what human beings can achieve in the best of all possible worlds.

But occasionally, it's good to hear of more mundane things because much of life is mundane, made up of ordinary little moments which, nevertheless, make up in sum a great deal of who we are. One of my college friends had a motto: "Don't sweat the small stuff." But the small stuff is important. And maybe some of it isn't quite so small after all. So here are a few of the small pieces of advice I intend to put into my next graduation speech:

Befriend a Kid

Graduates don't get to the point of being graduates without some encouragement along the way. It comes from relatives, teachers and principals, employers, ministers — in short, people we look up to partly because we think well of them, but partly because they just simply care about us. They tell us, often without putting it into so many words, that we're okay. They tell us that they expect good things from us. They invest time in us. They make us feel good about ourselves. And all of that is worth passing on.

Somewhere in every graduate's life there is a younger person who needs that kind of love and support. It may be a sibling, a kid in the neighborhood, a youngster across town. They keep an eye on people who are older than they are because that's how they learn about the world — by example. They need someone who's older — maybe even just a little bit older — to tell them they're unique and special and worthy, that they have talents and qualities worth developing, that they're okay. They need, in short, a good dose of self-esteem.

My advice to every graduate is to seek out at least one younger person and make it a point to invest some time in that kid. You don't have to take 'em to raise, just show some interest. And don't wait. Do it now. Form the habit. You'll find you get as much out of it as does the younger person. And who knows, you might even learn something in the process. In my case, I wouldn't have discovered the joy of Eric Clapton's music had a younger person not introduced me to it. And I do love to hear Eric Clapton sing.

Share Your Cake

My wife Paulette gets the credit for the notion of life as a kind of cake. She bakes well herself, but in this case she's talking about all the stuff we have and how we feel about it.

There's a certain minority of people in this world whose attitude is, "I've got my cake and you can't have any of it and I don't care if you get any of your own or not. Go away and let me eat my cake in peace."

Well, that's selfish and mean-spirited. And acting that way makes your soul wither up like a prune. Sharing your cake makes you feel larger, like the Biblical story of the loaves and fishes. The more Jesus gave away, the more there was. And he didn't stop to think about who deserved cake and who didn't. He gave unselfishly and unquestioningly. You can bet that in that crowd there was just about one of everything — saints and sinners, rich and poor, young and old, elegant and tacky. But Jesus made sure everybody got some cake and then they got down to business.

Be Disturbed

When we reach the point of graduation, we've been pumped full of other people's ideas for a long time. Parents, friends, teachers, gurus and commentators have all told us what they think. Now, it's time to figure out what *we* think. And we don't do that without a willingness to be disturbed.

I well remember my first semester in college, sitting in class and hearing ideas that were foreign to me — ideas that challenged a lot of what I had heard back home. It was like hearing that the world might be neither perfectly round nor exactly flat, but sort of oblong. That there was such a thing as shades of gray. That the best and worst of humanity could exist in a single human being. Some of those ideas made me angry. Some made me sad. Some made sense. All made me think, and that was the point. I was disturbed into thinking for myself and deciding what to keep and what to throw out and what to alter.

Belief is a good thing. But it doesn't hold a candle to conviction. Conviction is what we end up with when we've examined our beliefs and put them to the test of being challenged. It's what we get when we've gone through the process of being disturbed. And it's a lifelong process.

So there's some mundane stuff for the graduates. Diligence, integrity and commitment are good. So's the small stuff. It's worth sweating.

A Soldier, Far from Home

Thanksgiving is traditionally a family time, and I've been fortunate to spend all but one with my own family. The lone exception has made all the others more meaningful.

It was 1965. I was one of several thousand shaved-head recruits at Fort Jackson, South Carolina, where the United States Army was trying to turn out-of-shape, clumsy-footed civilians into lean, mean fighting machines. I was one of the older members of A Company, 10th Battalion, 2nd Regiment — just out of college, twenty-one years old, qualified by age to vote and order my own beer on a weekend pass in Columbia. Most of my fellow recruits were still teenagers, barely shaving.

Ray was one of the exceptions. I met him on

a Greyhound bus enroute to Fort Jackson. He got on in Atlanta, slipped into the seat next to mine, and struck up a conversation. We discovered that we had the same destination.

"Did you volunteer or get drafted?" I asked.

Ray laughed. "Neither. Well, I volunteered, but I had a little help from a judge." He went on to tell me that he was married with two small kids. He had lost his job at a service station. There wasn't any money. The kids were hungry. So Ray started writing bad checks. "What are you gonna do when the baby needs milk?" he asked. I didn't know how to answer that. I'd been raised not to write bad checks, but then I didn't have a wife and two kids at home and no job and no milk. Years later, when I did have a wife and two kids at home, I understood how a man might do a desperate thing in a desperate time.

Well, the cops came around to Ray's place one night, handcuffed him, put him in a squad car and took him to jail. The judge gave him a choice; he could serve more time in jail or he could join the Army. Back in those days, judges handed down choices like that to people who broke the law. I don't think they do that any more. But this judge did, and it sounded like a no-brainer to Ray. He sure wasn't going to be able to buy milk for the kids if he was in jail. And the Army meant a steady paycheck, with some extra for dependents. So the cops took him down to the Army recruiting office and got him signed up, and then they put him on the Greyhound.

Ray and I got assigned to the same basic training company — to the same platoon and squad, in fact. The Army made me the squad leader because I'd had a couple of years of ROTC in college. They gave me some squad leader's stripes and a dozen or so teenagers to take care of.

Teenagers, except for Ray, who was a year or two older than me and a whole lot wiser about the ways of the world. He should have been the squad leader. But he didn't care about stuff like that. What he cared about was his wife and his two kids back home in Atlanta. Those teenaged recruits in my squad were homesick, sure. But they weren't nearly as homesick as Ray.

Basic training started in late fall, and by the time Thanksgiving came, we were beginning to look a little like soldiers. The guys in the squad had formed a pretty tight group, and we were learning the essential lesson of soldiering — no matter who you are or where you come from, you'd better learn to depend on your buddies.

On the day before Thanksgiving, Ray pulled me off to the side and said, "I'm going AWOL. I can't stand it any more. I miss my wife and my kids and I'm going back to Atlanta."

"They'll stick your fanny in jail," I said.

"I don't care. I just don't think I can get through Thanksgiving without my family."

Maybe I shouldn't have, but I told the rest of the guys in the squad what Ray was contemplating. After chow that evening, when we had a little free time, we all gathered on the back steps of the barracks. And one by one, these guys from Puerto Rico and Pennsylvania and Colorado and Alabama told Ray how much we cared about him and how we didn't want him messing up his life. We'd be his family this one Thanksgiving, and maybe next year he'd be home in Atlanta with his real one.

The long and short of it is, Ray hung around. In the mess hall the next day, we had turkey and

dressing and cranberry sauce and the drill ser-
geants were halfway nice and all in all, it wasn't a
bad Thanksgiving if you had to be away from
home. Ray cried in his green beans, but the rest
of us started singing "Over the River and Through
the Woods" and that cheered him up a little.

I wish I could tell you that everything turned
out okay for Ray. But when basic training was
over and the Army gave us a two-week leave to go
home before advanced training began, Ray didn't
return. The Military Police picked him up and he
served some time in the stockade. What happened
after that, I don't know.

I do know that for one Thanksgiving, a few
young men — about as diverse a collection of humanity as you could round up — helped a friend
through a rough time. Families do that, even temporary families like the one we cobbled together
at Fort Jackson.

Every Thanksgiving, I think of Ray. I hope,
wherever he is, he's okay. And that he's got his
wife and his kids with him.

Random Acts of Kindness

One of the most intriguing people I've met
is Gene Chiosie, a police officer in West
Milford, New Jersey. I was hired a few years
ago to write a movie script about him. The movie
never got made, but it gave me a chance to know
Gene and his fascinating story, and to learn a les-

son about life and love that has stayed with me.

Gene was a truck driver back in the 1980's when his estranged wife and his best friend took Gene's two young children and disappeared. Gene spent ten agonizing years searching for them, and during that time he became a policeman. He thought it would help him in his search. It did a lot more than that.

Along the way, Gene discovered the worth of random acts of kindness. A fellow officer was telling him one day about his belief that the universe is one great cosmic balancing act. There are the laws of physics — action and reaction — which keep things from flying apart in all directions. And there's a similar law, this fellow said, that applies to the human condition. If you do a good deed, you may not see an immediate and proximate benefit to yourself. But somewhere else in the world, that good deed pays off. And if somebody else somewhere does something good, you may receive the blessing of it in a way you never expected. Action and reaction.

Gene believes it worked in his case. A police officer has all sorts of opportunities to do good deeds. He found police work rewarding and satisfying because he was able to give something of himself to people who needed it. And one day when he least expected it, something really good happened to him. He located his kids after a tip through a national television story and got them back.

There is, and always has been, plenty of evil in the world — people doing horrible things to other people. When you pick up the paper or watch the nightly news, you sometimes get the impression that there's nothing else, that evil is winning. But news is news, and often isn't reality in the broadest sense of the word. We know from our own everyday experience that there are an awful lot of good people in the world, doing lots of good things, often without thought of reward, even thanks. They do good things because it's simply the right thing to do, and the deed itself is the reward. Their good deeds, if Gene Chiosie's friend is right, even out the bad stuff. The cosmic balance is maintained. The universe can go on.

It's sort of a Boy Scout approach to life, I suppose. I remember from my Scouting days that if we were true to the ideals of Scouting, we were trustworthy, loyal, friendly, courteous, kind, obedient, cheerful, thrifty, brave, clean and reverent. I also remember that we were admonished to do at least one good deed every day. A random act of kindness.

There was the story of the Scoutmaster who was polling his troop on their kind acts for the day. One young fellow said he helped a little old lady across the street. "It took me fifteen minutes to get her across," the Scout said. Why? "She didn't want to go."

Sometimes the good deeds might be a little off the mark, but the important thing is that the heart is in the right place. The deed might be something pretty big, like the service project a young man plans and executes as part of the requirements for his Eagle Scout badge. But often, it's something really simple — like a smile and a hello. A Scout learns by performing those good deeds, large and small, to get into the habit of it. It becomes second nature. Scouts grow up to be those good people we know who are kind and thoughtful neighbors, dedicated police officers, teachers and nurses and ministers — and in general the sort of people who practice random acts of kindness.

We live not only in a world where there seems to be an overabundance of evil, but also where life proceeds at a breakneck pace. There never seems to be enough time to do the things that have to be done, much less time to pause for a good deed that doesn't seem to have an obvious payoff. We get caught up in the chaotic moment, the short view, the immediate frustration. We ride the bumper of the little old lady ahead of us on the highway, glaring and honking because she's making us late for the next thing that has to be done. Or we're irritable and abrupt in the check-out line. Or we hurry past the Salvation Army kettle at Christmas because if we hear just one more jangling bell, we're gonna lose it. An opportunity for a random act of kindness missed.

A friend says he once complained to his boss that he was working too hard and not getting enough rest. "You can rest the first five years you're dead," the boss replied. Maybe so. But you can't perform good deeds, random acts of kindness, after the lights go out. There's now, or there's never. If you don't believe it, ask Gene Chiosie.

All Nature Sings and Round Me Rings

He's not particularly religious, my neighbor tells me, but he considers himself spiritual. And why not? He's a man who's in constant contact, and in tune with, the natural world. And nature, if you give yourself to it, will sing to your spirit.

Like most of the men his age in the mountain valley where we spend some time, he went off to serve in World War Two, saw other parts of the world, and came back home to settle in the place that had nurtured him to manhood. He and his young wife bought fifty acres of land and used the fruits of it to raise and educate four children who have become successful adults. He tells of trapping muskrats to buy Christmas presents when the children were young. For the past couple of decades, he has grown Christmas trees in his fertile bottom land. He has spent most of his days outdoors, touching earth and sky and growing things and letting them touch him. In the evenings, he has read voraciously. He is a man of depth and understanding and keen insight, a thinker who has had the time and space to consider life below the surface, down where the secrets are. It has made him a spiritual man.

Now, spring has come to the mountains, and my neighbor and I are full of its vibrant awakening. We welcome it. We entice it.

Paulette and I are keeping an eye on the bird houses in our yard. They are as popular as a new condo complex at Myrtle Beach, but the prices are much better. We have chickadees in two of the units, Eastern bluebirds in two more, and our old friends the phoebes are nesting in a quiet corner of the front porch. One set of bluebirds has kept me particularly entertained. They came time and time again to a house near the window of my writing room, the lady a picky shopper who couldn't quite seem to make up her mind. Dad waits on the roof while Mom darts in and out of the house. "A fixer-upper," she says tentatively. "Yes, dear," he replies. "But a nice view." "Whatever you like, dear." He flies off to find a sale circular from Home Depot.

The thistle feeder is attracting a swarm of gold and purple finches. They perch in the branches of the maple tree nearby, waiting for a turn at the feeder, turning the maple into an Easter Egg tree of brilliant colors. Cardinals, titmice and nuthatches attack the sunflower feeder and the squirrels can gobble an ear of corn in an hour. Fuel for a busy day. Down by the river last week, we saw our first red-winged blackbird of the season.

The hummingbirds are back. I put the feeders out when the weather was dismal — damp and cold. An act of faith, I suppose. Within a few hours we had customers, the advance guard of the migration from the south, arriving ravenous from the long flight. (Humans aren't the only ones who complain about airline food.) They have taken over the porch now, darting and dogfighting over sugar water. We've had one casualty, a fellow who smashed into the glass of the door, apparently seeing his reflection and thinking it a rival. He was buried with honors.

The wild turkeys are about too, but they are discreetly shy this time of the year, tending their hidden homes and waiting for hatchlings. In another month we'll see parades of mothers and young across the gentle slope between house and river, nibbling at morsels in the grass. The young ones skitter about at mother's heels, watching to see what she does, where she goes. Kindergartners, learning the basics of turkey life.

I've never been able to understand atheists. How can you consider nature in all its rich, bursting diversity — so complex and yet so beautiful in its simplicity — and not feel the presence of a Creator? How can you look up at a clear night sky and not believe that there is Someone who knows the answers to all our questions? How can you, in other words, not be spiritual? For me, it's not necessary for belief to be based on blind faith. There's abundant evidence. I believe because I can see and touch and feel. Nature instructs me to be still and know.

In the Methodist church in my hometown, it was tradition for the young people to fill the choir loft periodically on Sunday nights and sing a special number while the ushers passed the offering plates. More often than not, we sang,
This is my Father's world
I rest me in the thought of rocks and trees and skies and seas
His hand the wonders wrought...
All nature sings and round me rings
The wonders of the spheres.

Occasionally I return to the sanctuary of that same little Methodist church and hear in my memory those tentative young voices singing a truth that we, in our innocence, were not yet perceptive or wise enough to appreciate. But we innocents were full of promise then, ripe for the world. Over the years, if we are fortunate, we have grown into knowledge and spirituality.

Spring can be our teacher. My neighbor knows. I'm learning.

The Great Bird Debate

E very year when Thanksgiving arrives, we make lists of things and people to be thankful for. Here's a name you might want to add: John Otis. Were it not for John, we might be eating eagles for Thanksgiving dinner.

John Otis was a Boston lawyer in 1771, when American patriots were beginning to talk about the nation they wanted to build after they wrested control of the colonies from King George. And one of the lofty issues they discussed was the designation of a national bird. Benjamin Franklin suggested the turkey. John Otis wanted the eagle. So they squared off in a public debate.

Both men were eloquent speakers who appreciated a good, spirited argument. Franklin's rhetorical gifts are well known. But Otis was no amateur himself. In fact, raising a ruckus seemed to run in his family. A relative, James Otis, was one of the most brazenly outspoken colonists in opposition to the oppressive acts of the British crown. James was reportedly the man who coined the phrase, "Taxation without representation is tyranny." James so incited the enmity of loyalists that in 1769, an officer of the crown attacked him with a cudgel. His injuries left him mentally incapacitated. So John took up the banner.

Both Ben Franklin and John Otis brought persuasive argument to the Great Bird Debate. Franklin championed the turkey because it had saved the Pilgrims from starvation during those first lean winters in Massachusetts. There would not be an America without the turkey, Franklin opined.

But Otis had history and nature on his side. The eagle has been a symbol of imperial power since Babylonian times. It is recognized as a fierce and proud bird. Eagles feed on live prey which they decapitate before devouring. *Bon appetit.* Not a bird to be trifled with.

Ben Franklin and John Otis debated over the birds for thirteen and a half hours. And when it was finished, Otis and the eagle were declared the winners. Aren't we glad? I imagine early Americans were, too. Thankful they didn't have to wrestle with whether or not to eat the national bird for Thanksgiving dinner. And thankful the ships of their young navy didn't have to sail the world with turkeys on their bows. Can you imagine the hoots from passing men-of-war?

Now, don't get me wrong about turkeys. They have my utmost respect. The turkey is sublime as a foodstuff, and he has gotten a bum rap over the years as a live creature.

The common wisdom on turkeys is that they are stupid. You've heard tales of domesticated turkeys standing in a rainstorm with their mouths open skyward, drinking until they drown. Maybe that's true. But in the wild, it is a different story.

I once went turkey hunting. I am not a hunter by nature, but a friend insisted that I fill that gap in my cultural development and even supplied me with a shotgun. We got up in the pitch black of a frigid winter pre-dawn, ate a hearty breakfast of grits, eggs, ham and red-eye gravy, donned several layers of clothing, hefted our trusty guns, and set off to kill turkeys.

The way you kill turkeys is to sit down in

the woods and call the turkeys with a little wooden device known as, of all things, a turkey call. So we sat down on the frozen ground and my friend called turkeys. For several hours. Dawn came. So did mid-morning, along with late morning and early afternoon. At that point, some other hunters came along. "The turkeys are over yonder," they said. We went over yonder. By the time we got there, the turkeys had left. This happened several other times during the afternoon. At nightfall we went home — cold, hungry, sore and empty-handed. "If turkeys are stupid," I thought, "what does that make me?"

On several occasions since that venture, I have seen real live wild turkeys. They showed themselves in plain view and gave me a good once-over before they took ungainly flight. They obviously knew I had no gun. Is that smart, or what?

All this is to say that Ben Franklin had a good point when he proposed the turkey as the national bird. Sometimes, I wish America's foreign policy was as clever as the turkey. Still, I rejoice in John Otis's victory in that 1771 debate. I honor the imperial eagle as a symbol of a proud nation. And I shall enjoy my Thanksgiving turkey in good health and high spirits, comforted by the knowledge that some other fool had to hunt the darn thing down.

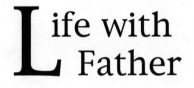

Life with Father

Defending Against the Under Toad

S he graduated from college and accepted a job in Chicago. A nice city, people kept tell ing us — vibrantly urban but pleasantly Midwestern. She would like Chicago, we were told. We hoped so, because Chicago was where she would begin the rest of her life, that life that belongs to her, not to us. She would make domestic arrangements, experience the triumphs and agonies of the workplace, perhaps meet the young man she couldn't do without. A life of her own. Exciting, of course, but perhaps a little scary, too, to be stepping off into a venture for which she was both prepared and clueless. She described her feelings as "bittersweet." I suppose that summed it up for all of us.

She is the younger of our two children, and we have been through this before. Our older daughter headed for Colorado as soon as she finished college. "Just a year to ski," she said. That was nine years ago. She fell in love with the young man she couldn't do without, a fine fellow from California, and they are firmly settled as Coloradans now with their own business and responsibilities and domestic arrangements. Paulette and I visit fairly often, and we have adapted to this long-distance relationship with an adult who is still our child.

So, we should have been prepared for what

this younger daughter was about to embark upon. Except that we weren't. We were exquisitely proud of her, of the lovely, smart, personable young woman she had become. We were delighted that she had found a job that would challenge and reward her. But there was an element of something else. Perhaps grief is too strong a word, but it hints at what we felt. Perhaps it has something to do with the Under Toad.

Writer John Irving introduced the notion in his 1978 novel, *The World According to Garp.* The family of T.S. Garp vacations every summer on the coast of New Hampshire where the Atlantic can be made treacherous by a vicious riptide. "Watch out for the undertow," an older brother tells a younger. "What can it do to you?" the younger boy asks. It can suck you under and drown you and drag you away. One day, the family finds the younger boy standing at water's edge, staring intently into the surf. When they ask him what he's doing, he says he's trying to see the Under Toad, imagining a giant toad lurking offshore, waiting to grab the ankles of an unsuspecting bather. To Garp and his wife, the Under Toad becomes their code phrase for anxiety.

Every parent fears the Under Toad, that legion of perils, real and imagined, that lurk in the shadows of our child-raising experience — disease and accident, molesters and abductors — anything that threatens the innocent young with whose health and safety we have been entrusted. We wish to shield them from all harm, all disappointment, all sorrow. As they grow, becoming their own persons and taking on greater responsibility for themselves, we learn painfully to give up a little, to let go a little at a time. But along the way, we try to do all in our power to protect them and prepare them. We talk, we listen, we advise, we take precautions. Wear your helmet when you ride your bike. Don't swim right after lunch. Don't talk to strangers. We do all we can, but we're never very far from our fears. It's part of the job. Life with the Under Toad.

Perhaps one of the subtler and more devious acts of the Under Toad is the theft of innocence, the revelation that the world can be a cruel and unforgiving place. The news reporter asks a student who survived the bloodbath at Columbine High School in Littleton, Colorado, how the experience changed her. "It made me realize how fragile life can be," she replies. It's true, life can be fragile. But how sad to see that so brutally brought home to an 18-year-old, at a time when we would wish life to be all hope and optimism. Littleton reminds every parent that the Under Toad lurks just beneath what may seem to be a calm sea. We pray that it will spare us. As John Irving writes in another of his novels, "The grief of lost children never dies."

But to be a parent is not to surrender to despair. There is an inevitable time of turning loose, of sending the young from the nest to seek their own way and become their own uniqueness. We do them no favor if we cling too hard and too long. Rather, we try to prepare them for life by letting them know that there is much good in the world, much to celebrate and strive for. We show them by our example the concepts of faith and fairness and kindness. They will have to deal with their own Under Toads at some point along the way, but we teach them that they have strong defenses — love and caring and reasonable precaution.

So, she left us — first for Chicago, and then

on to Birmingham. We can no longer protect her from the Under Toad, if in fact we ever could. She left, but in one sense she will always be close by. As she ventures into the world, Under Toad and all, she takes some of us with her — all that investment that we made from the beginning. Bittersweet, yes. But not final. We know how to find the Chicagos and Birminghams of the world. And she knows how to find home.

The Girl I Couldn't Do Without

When Valentine's Day approaches, as the old saying goes, a young man's fancy turns to what the young ladies have been thinking about all year. It's time for pledges of love and devotion, hearts and flowers. And many a young couple choose the occasion to make what they intend as a permanent commitment. For them, I pass along the best piece of advice my mother ever gave me: marry the one you can't do without.

It was exciting and fun to be young and single in Montgomery, Alabama, in the mid-sixties. The town was full of people like me, just beginning adult lives and careers. We dated, partied, and frequently paired off. It was a time and place in which marriage was at least in the back of most young minds.

For the most part, I tried to remain a moving target. So many girls, so little time. But occasionally, things would progress beyond mere dating and I would take a girl home to meet my parents. It was after one of those visits that my mother said to me, "Marry the girl you can't do without." I asked myself the question every time a relationship got down to the nitty-gritty: "Can I do without this one?" Invariably, the answer was, "Yes." Then I met Paulette Strong. She was pretty, smart, classy and fun. But there was something more. Something indefinable. She was, I realized, the girl I couldn't do without.

I moved quickly, because Miss Strong was being hotly pursued by a number of other young Montgomery swains. We had our first date the weekend after Thanksgiving. On the following Groundhog Day, I proposed. On April 15th, we married. That was more than thirty years ago.

We knew we were making progress when we outlasted the first set of major appliances. The TV set, the washer and dryer, the refrigerator all died. The marriage went on. A second set of appliances is beginning to get long in the tooth. And Paulette is still the girl I can't do without. Without her, I would not be whole. It's love, but more than that.

Maybe my mother's standard is a tough way to judge a prospective wife or husband. But a marriage has to stand up to a lot, and I guess it's better to be tough going in than tough going out. The thing about a marriage is, there's no place to hide. If the one you see across your coffee cup every morning isn't the one you just couldn't do without, the relationship may not handle the rough spots.

I've passed along my mother's advice to several young friends who were of marriageable age and stage and were in the throes of acute romantic agony. I've had the privilege of witnessing several of their weddings. In each case, the bride was beautiful and the groom was handsome, as all brides and grooms are. But there was more. In each case, bride and groom knew there was something special. You could see it in their eyes. They were marrying the one they couldn't do without.

A marriage, of course, is based on more than need. And it takes constant care and grooming. The pressures of money, kids, parents, society, and temptation intrude on our marriages. Even the very strongest face crises. Sometimes we feel like smoke-jumpers, parachuting into a burning forest. The thing is, I guess, to hold hands and jump together. When we emerge, soot-stained and singed, it's important to remember why we started out together in the first place.

One good friend, a little older than I, told me recently that he and his wife of many years have rediscovered the joy of romancing each other. Gee, that's nice. In doing so, they rediscover daily the reason they can't do without each other.

I read an interview the other day with a bachelor who said he was waiting for the perfect girl. I don't believe there is one, or a perfect guy either. But if you find the one you can't do without, that's as near perfect as we can expect love to be.

Mother was right.

Singing the Atlanta Interstate Blues

I'm rocketing along on Interstate 285, Atlanta's outerbelt freeway, me and several thousand other souls, facing death like a man and listening to Alison Krauss on the CD player.

Oh Atlanta, I hear you calling.
I'm coming back to you one fine day....

I'm here because I have no choice. Folks across the South used to say that to go to hell, you had to pass through the Atlanta airport. Nowadays, that pretty much holds true for I-285. And I've been on I-285 enough times in my life to have a pretty good idea what hell is like.

This time I am on a book promotion tour, shamelessly hawking my novels, art meeting commerce. I'm enroute from a bookstore appearance in Birmingham, headed to another on the northside Atlanta suburb of Snellville. I can take I-285 or I can detour through Kentucky and the Carolinas.

I don't have time for a detour. So I'm driving I-285 with my usual white-knuckled terror and listening to Alison Krauss's song about Atlanta. It has a great beat to it, but she probably wrote it in a room in the Peachtree Plaza hotel. She darn sure didn't write it on I-285.

No need to worry,
Ain't no hurry....

Hurry? These folks out here on I-285 invented the word. Once upon a time, I-285 was two lanes in each direction. It quickly filled up with cars and the state of Georgia started adding lanes. Now, I'd wager it has more square yards of concrete than the rest of the Atlanta metropolitan area combined, so many lanes in each direction that I've lost count. And it's still filled up with cars. The slow ones are exceeding the speed limit by twenty or so miles an hour.

Except at rush hour, that is, when I-285 is, in many places, a giant parking lot. It is the only place on earth I've ever seen people in a hurry when they are at a dead standstill. Thousands of drivers, drumming their fingers on the steering wheel, edging forward impatiently at the merest hint of space between them and the vehicle just ahead.

Most of the time, drivers on I-285 are both in a hurry and going very fast. Defensive driving here is pedal-to-the-metal, horn-honking, sheet-metal-trading madness that would get you a stiff fine in a NASCAR race. But there seem to be no fines here. There seem to be no cops. The prevailing advice from law enforcement authorities appears to be, "Y'all be careful now, y'heah."

I've been driving I-285 from its modest beginning, shuttling between home in North Carolina and relatives in Alabama, usually with wife and children in the car. The two girls occupied the back seat, and for most of the trip it was a chorus of "She touched me!" But when we hit Atlanta everybody shut up upon pain of death. It was always a grim passage, and when we were safely back on I-85 headed for Montgomery or I-20 toward Birmingham, Dad stopped for a long bathroom break.

I'm going back, back to Georgia....

Alison Krauss makes it sound so benign. And for the most part, Georgia is. It's really one of my favorite states — from the north Georgia hills to the piney woods of the coastal plains. There is, to much of Georgia, a genteel softness that I associate with good manners and an appreciation for time and place. My first novel was turned into a movie in a small Georgia town. Our older daughter graduated from college in Athens. I still hold a bit of a grudge against General Sherman.

Atlanta, likewise, is one of my favorite cities. Back in the dark days at mid-century when the South was struggling with its demons of race and ignorance, Atlanta seemed to find a way to solve problems and keep moving. It was the south's City on the Hill, Lester Maddox notwithstanding. I was among the legions of Southerners who rejoiced with pride when Atlanta was awarded the 1996 Olympics. It seemed to say that we were, after all, okay.

So I like Georgia and I like Atlanta. But I do not like I-285.

In my briefcase now, I have a clipping that I snipped from my local paper just before I left home on my book tour. It says my fellow novelist Anne Rivers Siddons is leaving Atlanta, her lifelong home, for Charleston. She blames "traffic jams and unbridled development." If Anne is lucky, she'll never have to travel I-285 again.

I also have a clipping that tells how a Charlotte politician called that city's planned outerbelt freeway a "circular plague of locusts" and said the city ought to think about maybe not building it.

I'll bet a lot of folks thought that politician was smoking loco weed when he said that. At this moment, here on I-285 in Atlanta, he sounds like the soul of wisdom.

Oh Atlanta, I hear you calling....
Sing it, Alison. Sing it, honey.

To a Son-in-law, Contemplating Fatherhood

Dear Chris,
 "I heard the heartbeat," you said. And the way you said it, with such a mixture of awe and wonder, let me know that this business of impending fatherhood is something so special, so unique, so humbling, that it's impossible to truly put into words. It tells me you're going to be a fine father. But then, I already knew that, because you're a fine fellow. You love my daughter, and that alone makes you okay in my book.

What is a father's hope for a daughter? That, when she chooses a partner, she'll pick someone who cherishes her as much as her father does. Cherish. Now, there's a pretty big word. It means you not only love someone, you cling to them, protect them, nurture them, honor them, give them the best that is in yourself. Well, my daughter found someone to truly cherish her, someone she can cherish in return. And now the two of you, after careful thought, have decided to bring new life into the world — someone both of you will cherish, as you do each other.

Larkin says you're even more excited about the big event than she is. That says a lot, because she's pretty excited. I'm glad the two of you share that, because it means you're also comfortable with the awesome responsibility that you assume when you become a parent.

Enjoy your excitement, and don't fret if at times you feel a little left out of this process. Pregnancy is not a guy thing. A guy sort of helps launch the boat and then watches it sail away without him. A woman is a mother from the moment of conception. A father has to wait for birth, and in the meantime, content himself with things like listening to the heartbeat and painting the bedroom.

I realized this during Paulette's two pregnancies, and I wrote about it in a novel a few years ago. My character Bright Birdsong was pregnant, and her husband, Fitzhugh, "clucked and fussed about her, trying to *do* something, anything ... captivated by her changing body — touching, listening, poking gently, asking a thousand questions."

Hosanna, the family housekeeper, a woman of vast native wisdom, tells Bright, "He can't help it. Biggest thing a man ever do is begat. Every time a woman get with child, you see the man struttin' around like a peahen, 'cause he done begat. Hell, ain't nothin' to begattin'. It's after the begattin' that you gets down to bidness. And it drive the man near about crazy 'cause he can't run the bidness."

No, we guys can't run the bidness. But we can ponder on what happens after the bidness — the birthing — is done. Because that's where *our* real bidness begins, that thing called fatherhood.

I'm sure there are some good books about fatherhood, probably even some classes you can take. I always just played it by ear, letting the experience unfold day by day, applying lessons I had learned from watching other fathers — some positive lessons, some negative. I made a lot of mistakes along the way, but apparently not terminal ones. I'm fortunate that our two girls have a wonderful mother who smoothed over my mistakes and did the best of the parenting in our family. It must have all worked pretty well, because the girls turned out to be fine young women.

I didn't have any rules as I went along learning how to be a father, but looking back on it, there were a few principles that I seem to have followed.

Love for a child is unconditional. A son or daughter may sometimes disappoint you, make you angry, defy you, ignore your advice. Whatever. But those times are simply an opportunity to remember that your love for your child isn't something that's parceled out or measured. It has no limitations. It's just always there.

It's okay to have expectations. We're all children at heart, and we all do better when we know where the boundaries are, what the rules are, what's expected of us. Your son or daughter might not always *do* what you want, but if he or she doesn't *know* what you want, what you expect, it darn sure won't happen.

Fathers change diapers. You can't really appreciate fatherhood until you get it on you.

But I really don't need to tell you all this. You'll figure it out for yourself. You'll do just fine as a father because you've got solid instincts, a good notion of what's right and wrong, a great capacity for love, and a profound sense of responsibility.

Our daughter is in good hands, Chris, and our grandchild will be, too. Paulette and I will be there to support without meddling, to enjoy the special relationship that exists between grandparent and grandchild. But this is your show, yours and Larkin's. Let the games begin.

Love, Bob

The Joys of the Directionally Challenged

The Cajun humorist Justin Wilson used to tell the story of a fellow in a big Cadillac who pulled up to a rural Louisiana intersection, rolled down his window, and asked a boy who was standing at the roadside, "Son, if I keep going in this direction, where will I be?"

"I don't rightly know," the boy said.

"Well, if I turn left, where will that take me?"

"Don't know that, either.

"And if I turn right?"

"Beats me, mister."

His exasperation growing, the fellow in the Cadillac asked, "What if I turn around and head back where I came from?"

The boy just shrugged.

"Well, you don't know a dang thing, do you?" the fellow said.

"No sir, but then I ain't lost, either."

I thought about that story when I saw an advertisement for an automobile with an on-board satellite computer system. In this particular automobile, if you need assistance out on the road anywhere, you just press a button and a real live human being speaks up and says, "May I help you, Mr. Jones?" If your car has broken down, the real live human being will send a tow truck and a limousine to pick you up and whisk you to the nearest authorized repair shop. The real live human also performs other services ranging from advising you on the nearest good French restaurant to ordering Super Bowl tickets. All well and good. Modern technology in service of mankind. But there is one thing about this system I believe is bad business: it gives directions when you are lost.

I say this from a male perspective. As we all know, men and women are different, and thanks be to the Creator for that. The difference in men and women makes for all sorts of delicious possibilities. But the one difference that is a ready-made recipe for conflict is that men hate asking for directions.

Witness this exchange between a husband and wife on a two-lane road somewhere in rural Iredell County, North Carolina, enroute to the Union Grove Pig Pickin' Festival:

Wife: "Are you lost?"

Husband: "Of course not. I know exactly where I am."

Wife: "Then why did you hesitate at that last intersection?"

Husband: "I was just taking a brief nap."

Wife: "You're lost."

Husband: "Will you just read your soap opera magazine and let me drive?"

Wife: "Why don't you pull over and ask somebody for directions?"

Husband: "I don't need directions."

Wife: "I think we just passed Raleigh."

Eventually, our husband and wife will arrive in Union Grove. It may be by a somewhat circuitous route, and it may take several days to get there. But if our husband is any kind of red-blooded, true-blue American male, he will never ask for directions, admit he has been the least bit lost, or apologize for the soap opera magazine remark.

Imagine the same conversation in one of these new automobiles with the on-board satellite computer system.

Wife: "Do you know where you are?"

Husband: "Of course."

Wife: "No you don't, you're lost."

Wife presses button, activating on-board satellite computer system.

Female Voice: "May I help you, Mr. Jones?"

Husband: "NO!"

Wife: "He's lost again."

Female Voice: "Third time this week, Mrs. Jones. Men. What are we gonna do with 'em?"

You have here, obviously, the makings of a major domestic crisis. No, ladies, we often don't know where we are. But dang it, we're perfectly comfortable with our ignorance. It is the male prerogative to use our cleverness, intuition and charm to get us out of tight places. We're all a bit like General Custer: "Those Indians must be around here someplace." We are the hunter-gatherers of society. We gather our wits and hunt for places. That fellow in Justin Wilson's story was an aberration. Probably one of those in-touch-with-my-inner-self types.

Didn't Moses lead the Children of Israel out of bondage? He probably didn't have the foggiest idea where he was headed, but he eventually got there with a little help from God, who conveniently parted the Red Sea. "Ah," said Moses. "A super-highway. Let's try this." Ever since, men have counted on Divine Providence to lead them out of all sorts of wildernesses, many of their own making.

I predict a rebellion against this new-fangled technology of on-board satellite computer systems in automobiles. The cars may sell, but don't be surprised if you see them around town with nothing but female occupants.

Watching the Phoebe:
A Parenthood Lesson

S pring in the High Country. Our phoebes have arrived and they're back in business. For the past several years, we've been watching and enjoying a particular pair of eastern phoebes who have apparently adopted us. We assume, or at least hope, it's the same pair. They keep using the same nest perched on a beam beneath our porch over-hang — a bird condominium now in its fourth sea-son. Each year about this time it gets a modest redecorating and then family life begins.

I've been reading about eastern phoebes and I've found them to be interesting bird folk. The phoebe is a country fellow, at home in fields and streamsides. He isn't much for looks — a chunky, brownish-gray body with a slightly darker head. But he is a purposeful, energetic bird. When our particular pair arrive, they inspire us to all man-ner of spring activity — planting, trimming, win-dow-washing and the like.

Our porch is typical as a nesting place. Phoe-bes prefer quiet corners, under the eaves of a shed or under a bridge. Our log house apparently looks sufficiently shed-like to qualify.

The nest itself is constructed with moss and strengthened with mud, a regular little fortress, glued firmly to the beam and protected from wind, rain and predators. We have a lot of crows in the neighborhood, and local wisdom says the crows rob the nests of other birds. But I defy a crow to get near this nest. There just isn't room for his big, gawky frame under the overhang.

Phoebes spend the winter in warmer climes,

mainly in the Gulf Coast states, then begin a late-winter migration northward. The reason is their diet — almost exclusively insects, available in abundance only after snow is gone. It's not unusual to spot them in early spring as far north as Maine, especially when there's been a mild winter. Before long, phoebes will be settling in for the summer throughout the Eastern and Midwestern U.S. and into much of Canada.

But for now, our particular pair of phoebes have stopped off to raise a brood of young. At the moment, they're in the redecorating phase. As I sit looking out my upstairs window, one of them is perched on a high branch of a budding maple tree, tail bobbing up and down in typical phoebe fashion, scanning the landscape for just the right piece of moss or daub of mud. Do male and female phoebe shop together? I think perhaps not, avoiding the possibility of argument. But each seems perfectly satisfied with whatever the other brings to the project.

Shortly, we will have eggs in the nest, and then babies, and days of furious parental activity. Once the hatching is done, mother and father will swoop about the yard spearing insects in mid-air and carrying them back to the three or four young who crowd the nest, scrawny demanding beaks thrust raucously skyward. Mother and father seem to share equally in the work.

The phoebe couple don't seem to mind their human neighbors. If we walk out onto the porch, whoever is busy at the nest will fly away. Then they wait patiently for us to leave and get back to business. I suspect that they believe the house actually belongs to them, and that we are the amiable visitors. When they eventually fly off to join Uncle Izzy in the Catskills for the summer, they may imagine us making a similar pilgrimage to Cleveland or Presque Isle.

For the moment, we peacefully co-exist here in the mountains, entirely comfortable with each other's presence. The birds are busy with their family affairs, while the fellow who lives inside the house taps on his computer and emerges periodically to join his missus digging in the dirt. We ask little of each other. The humans are satisfied to watch the intimate drama of bird-parenting. And the birds are happy as long as there are plenty of insects. A nice life all around.

The phoebes share their domesticity with us in every instance but one. They have never let us see their young take flight, as other species commonly do. We watch diligently as the babies grow to fluffy balls of feather and our anticipation mounts as they battle each other for elbow room in the nest. Then one morning we will walk onto the porch to find them gone. It has been done quietly and unobtrusively, a private family business to which we are not invited nor, no doubt, welcome.

As this year's drama begins, I am wondering already about that inevitable rite of passage that will be its final curtain. What do bird parents tell their young when they leave the nest? Perhaps it is this: *I have given you all I am and have. I have done the best I could. Now, go and thrive.*

It would seem to be enough.

The One in My Family Who Really Counts

I jokingly tell people that I married my wife because she could count and she married me because I could spell. There's a grain of truth in that, but it doesn't begin to count the ways, no pun intended. I married Paulette because she is — among other things — beautiful, warm-hearted, generous, even-tempered, talented and witty. But in truth, Paulette's ability to count counts for a lot.

When I was a single man, just starting off in the world of work, I was paid a pittance by my employer. It was important for me to know where every dime went because there just weren't that many dimes. But I was, to put it bluntly, numerically impaired. When I took that first job, I promptly opened a checking account at a bank. And within weeks, I was utterly clueless about how much money was in it. I knew there wasn't much — but how much? Clueless.

Being clever in things besides numbers, I went across town to another bank and opened an account there. I began to deposit paychecks in that account and write checks upon it while all the checks on the first account cleared and I could find out what was left and close out the account. Every few months or so, I opened a new checking account. By the time I married, I was running out of banks.

My mother was appalled at my ineptitude. She taught bookkeeping at the high school level, and had a good head for numbers. At our house, she handled the finances. Alas, I took after my father who once said, "There are three kinds of people in the world: those who can count and those who can't." Mother tried to teach me to balance a checkbook. I think it was the only time she used the word "dummy" in my presence.

Then along came Paulette. She could count. As we were courting, I discovered all sorts of amazing things about her — among them, that her checkbook was in pristine condition. Like me, she didn't have much in it, but she knew what she had. For my part, I was a wordsmith — a young journalist at the time, interpreting events large and small to an eager and appreciative public. I've always been able to spell. Words sing to me and tell me instinctively when an "e" should go before an "i" and vice versa.

So we formed a partnership — based, partly, on our complementary talents. In many ways, we are opposites. But we seem to fit, and have for more than thirty years.

After the nuptials, we talked about finances. We decided that I would pay the bills, since I knew how to spell the names of our creditors, and Paulette would balance the checkbook. It worked. And then when income tax time rolled around (it's always easy to remember our anniversary because we married on April 15th) lo' and behold Paulette filled out our tax return. I was in awe and took her out for a nice dinner.

Several years ago, I acquired a computer to aid me in my writing chores. And on this computer I eventually placed a marvelous piece of software that keeps track of finances. I use it for recording who owes what and what gets paid. And at the end of each month, when the bank statement comes in, this marvelous piece of software *balances the checkbook.* I have been able to relieve Paulette of that burden, and it has brought me — the ultimate numbers klutz — no small measure of satisfaction.

I was graphically reminded of my ineptitude with figures when the computer died. The hard drive crashed, not with a bang, but with a whimper. The data was saved, but for several days while the computer was being fixed, I was without my crutch, consigned again to the netherworld of the numerically impaired.

Once again, I am reminded that I am married to a wonderful woman who can count. If she ever leaves me, she might as well take all the money. I wouldn't know what to do with it anyway.

The Power of Great Expectations

Interesting how you can re-discover a powerful influence on your life, long after you had forgotten it existed.

On a visit home to Alabama a few years ago, I rummaged through a box that I had packed away after college and stored in my parents' attic. I found a book of devotionals, a high school graduation gift from my Sunday School teacher who was a dear sweet lady named Cammie Johnson. In the flyleaf of the book, she had inscribed the words, "Bobby, don't ever let me down."

It occurred to me, as I leafed through the

book years later, that Mrs. Johnson's admonition was a pretty big burden to put on the shoulders of a young man as he left for college. The University of Alabama was known in 1961 as one of the premier party schools of the nation. I changed my name from Bobby to Bob, joined a social fraternity, and proceeded to socialize. There were times I made a fool of myself, as college students will do.

In the years since, I've done foolish things on a fairly regular basis. But I am still married to the same woman I wed more than thirty years ago and have no felony convictions. So I suppose I've made some right choices when faced with moral dilemmas. I should give some of the credit to Cammie Johnson. Maybe, in the greater scheme of things, I really didn't let her down.

If it takes an entire village to raise a child, my village raised me. I grew up in a town where the grownups took a genuine interest in young folks. They said by their actions that they loved us and cared about us. And they let us know in no uncertain terms that they expected us to always do the right thing. We didn't, of course, but when we did the wrong thing, we knew it was wrong, and we felt a little guilty.

I thought about Cammie Johnson and the business of expectations when I read that police officers who work in our schools have been given a new mission: talking to teenagers about not drinking or using drugs. They have their work cut out for them. A recent survey found that sixteen percent of eighth graders nationwide are binge drinkers. That means they consume five or more drinks at a sitting. Seventy percent of high school students in one Southern state say they use alcohol. The figures are climbing and the danger is growing: fatal accidents and antisocial behavior now, wrecked marriages and ruined careers later.

A few days before the story about binge drinking, there was another about a new study on the effect adults have on teenage behavior. The conclusion is dramatic, if adults exercise it.

The survey polled 12,000 seventh-through-twelfth graders nationwide. These kids said unequivocally that the more they feel loved by their parents, the less likely they are to have early sex, smoke, abuse booze or drugs, or commit violence or suicide. The researchers found that if parents expected teenagers to get good grades, avoid substance abuse and refrain from sex, those expectations had a powerful influence on the kids' behavior. And that's true regardless of the race or income of the parents, and whether there's one or two parents in the home.

Teenagers like to complain about their parents, and the litany hasn't changed much over the years: parents are over-protective, old-fashioned, and downright embarrassing. The problem comes when parents believe it.

When our older daughter was in junior high, she had a good friend who was, to put it mildly, a handful. Her parents were concerned, but fatalistic. The mother told my wife Paulette, "When they reach a certain age, there's just not much you can do with them." Paulette thought that was a bunch of bull-hockey. She was the drill sergeant at our house, and she believed that there *was* a lot you could do. For one thing, you could say "no." We said "no" a lot, and we always tried to present a united front. Our daughter had her squirrelly moments, but she didn't turn out to be a hooligan. In fact, she turned out pretty darn well.

I think it really is okay to say "no," to have rules and consequences and expectations. The teenagers may fume and chafe, but a lot of that is for peer group consumption. Deep down, they're saying in this survey, they welcome boundaries and involvement in their lives, even when it's inconvenient. Adolescent hormones don't purge the human body and spirit of the need to be loved and nurtured.

We shouldn't need police officers in our schools breaking up fights, making arrests, and warning against drugs and alcohol. But we do, because not enough of that is happening at home.

We can change things by giving our young folk our unconditional love and our unwavering expectations. Like Cammie Johnson did for me.

Everything I Need to Know I learned at the Grocery Store

I am in the checkout line at the grocery store. A lot of people call these things supermarkets, but for me personally, there's nothing super about the supermarket. Especially today.

The place is jammed. It's early on a Wednesday evening (usually, in my experience, an off-time for grocery shopping). There's been no forecast of snow. Nobody's trying to stock up before dashing home to catch a football game on TV. But there are so many people in the grocery store, I expect to see the fire marshal. It's as if everybody within several miles of the store got an emergency phone message: *Get food!* Or maybe it's one of those subliminal things they flash on your TV screen so fast you don't realize what's hit you. Like the ones that say, "FLOURIDE IS A COMMU- NIST PLOT." Whatever the reason, we are all here and we are all looking pretty intense, probably because we are all here.

I am in the express checkout line. There are perhaps twnety of us here and there is nothing express about it. The lady at the counter has one item, a quart of ice cream. This particular brand and size of ice cream has a special low price if you have your Super Duper Saver Card. Our customer's card is at home. But she's haggling with the clerk, insisting that she get the special low price nonetheless. The clerk is patiently ex- plaining that unless he enters her Super Duper Saver Card number in the computer, it will not ring up the sale price. The argument drones on. The customer is offended. The clerk is weary. Some of the other people in the express line are beginning to get rowdy. I decide to remain calm.

I look for something to distract me. There is a rack of magazines and newspapers next to the checkout line — placed there, of course, for just such occasions. I select a tabloid. The front page story tells about a woman who had her head sev- ered in surgery and then re-attached. It seems she had a tumor on the upper end of her spinal column and the surgeons decided the easiest way to remove it was to take off her head. The sur- gery was imminently successful, the woman has made a full recovery and will soon resume play- ing ice hockey. As I reach the end of the story, I learn that the operation took place in Sweden. Darn, I think, why don't interesting things like that

ever happen where I live? All these terrific surgeons in town, and nobody's tried head-severing.

I'm about to flip to the next incredible story
in the tabloid when the conversation of two women
just ahead of me catches my attention. One of
them attended a big craft show the previous weekend, and in line ahead of her at the concession
stand was an extremely pregnant woman. As the
woman was about to place her order, her water
broke. "Well, did they rush her to the hospital?"
"No, she ordered some nachos and shopped awhile
longer."

I put down the tabloid. This is so much better. Incredible things *do* happen where I live. Why
are stories like this never in the local paper? Do
we need a local tabloid? Or should we spend more
time standing in checkout lines at the grocery store
to learn what's *really* going on?

Speaking of the checkout line, it has moved
a bit. The woman with the ice cream has stormed
off, leaving her quart melting on the counter.
Another customer is moving up. He has at least
twenty items and has a look on his face that tells
the clerk, "Don't give me this ten-item malarkey,
buster. I had a tough day at work." The clerk
begins ringing him up. After every item has been
entered in the computer and the sale totaled, *then*
the customer pulls out his checkbook. If he's out
of checks, I think, he's a dead man. But no, he has
checks. He writes one. Laboriously. But he has
no identification. His wallet is in the car. His gro-
ceries are confiscated by two hulking bag boys
while he retrieves the wallet.

If I had a flip phone, I'd call home and tell
my wife I'll be delayed. But I don't own a flip
phone, so I sigh and settle in. I watch a parent
chase a small child who refuses to give up the jar

of pickled pigs' feet he has snatched from a shelf. If the kid wants pigs' feet, let him have it.

I reflect on what I consider the ill-conceived layout of grocery stores. Beer should be next to pretzels. Milk should be next to cereal. But they aren't. I usually do more wandering than shopping, trying to find what I need without asking stupid questions. "Where's the beef?" "Right behind you, sir. It's that red stuff."

It's dark outside. But nothing important is going on out there. We're all in here. The express line now stretches around the deli counter and down toward the yogurt. I pick up the tabloid again. At least I'm reading and hearing the news I need to know.

Floating to Earth on Faith

When William Miley died, I lost a godfather. I never met him, never even knew him by name. But my father was a paratrooper, and William Miley was the father of U.S. Army paratroopers. So he's sort of a godfather to me because paratroopers are a vivid memory of my childhood.

In the years between the world wars, the American military had no interest in parachute tactics. But when Germany launched highly successful airborne operations in 1940, the Pentagon took notice. Miley was picked to organize the Army's first parachute unit, and he was a division commander when the Allies mounted massive airborne assaults during World War Two. He started the tradition that a paratroop commander always jumps into action with his troops, instead of directing things from the rear.

My father came to the business later. He was a World War Two veteran, called back to duty for the Korean Conflict. I don't know what got into him. He was in his early thirties with a wife and four small children, but he volunteered for just about every dangerous assignment the Army had to offer. He went to parachute school, trained to become a Ranger, and then became one of the original members of the elite Special Forces. It must have scared the willies out of my mother. I thought it was pretty neat.

If I had known what Dad was doing in Korea, it probably would have scared me, too. I learned later that his unit, the 10th Special Forces Group, set up a base just south of Seoul where they trained South Korean troopers in guerilla warfare. Then they went north and wreaked havoc.

Their cover was typically a B-29 bombing raid on a target in North Korea. All of the B-29's carried bombs except for the last one in the flight. Its bomb bay was sealed shut and a hole cut in the floor. Sitting around the hole were my Dad, another American, and a group of ten or so South Koreans. The other B-29's dropped their bombs, and then Dad's group parachuted out. Once on the ground, they blew up a bridge or an ammunition dump, then high-tailed it to the coast where the Navy picked them up. Once, Dad's group got captured. They got away. He never would talk much about it, but I got the impression it was a nasty affair.

After the war, he stayed in the Army for several years, always with an airborne unit, always at posts in the South — Fort Bragg, Fort Benning, Fort Campbell. Every chance he got, he strapped on his parachute and jumped. He had to do it at least once a month to get his extra "jump pay." I think he would have done it twice a day if they had let him.

There was and is a fraternity among paratroopers akin to that of pilots — a company of strong-willed men who go in harm's way. There is a grim, often macabre humor about them, an ability to laugh in the face of death.

The old troopers, my Dad's buddies, told the story of the young soldier nervously facing his first jump. "Don't worry," his sergeant said, "the Army will take care of you. When you jump, the static line that's attached to the plane will automatically open your main chute. If for some reason that fails, you have an emergency chute strapped to your chest. Just pull the ripcord and you'll float safely to earth. A truck will be waiting to bring you back to the barracks."

The young trooper jumped. The static line broke. He reached for the ripcord on his emergency chute and it came off in his hand. As he hurtled toward earth, he yelled up at the plane, "Yeah, and I'll bet that truck ain't there, either."

Our family often went to watch Dad jump out of airplanes. As we stood on the edge of the drop zone, a swarm of lumbering C-121 transport planes — "Flying Boxcars," the troopers called them — would appear overhead. Then tiny dots would begin to stream from the open doors and chutes would pop open and soon the sky was filled with hundreds of men, floating to earth on faith. It was a breathtaking sight, the stuff of wonder and myth.

My Dad battled demons in those days, and they finally drove him out of the Army. But for those precious moments when he was suspended between sky and earth, I believe he was a free man. Demons aren't brave enough to jump out of an airplane.

Sometimes, in my dreams, I am a paratrooper. I leap into space with nothing to save me but faith in the billowing expanse of silk that I ride gently to earth. It is quiet up there, nothing but the rush of wind through shroud lines. I am, for an exquisite moment, free. And the truck is always waiting to take me home.

On the Nature of Boys and Girls

S unday afternoon in the mountains. A warm, sun-splashed day with nothing in particular to do except — as my grandmother used to call it — "marinate." She thought that life, like a good piece of beef, was better if you let it soak awhile before you set it on fire. So I am on the porch marinating, absorbing the sights and sounds and spices of the afternoon. And I am ruminating on the nature of boys and girls.

There are the hummingbirds. We have two small feeders hung above the porch banister, each with three feeding places. Six watering holes for the five birds who are the afternoon visitors to refuel their tiny supercharged bodies. No need to push and fuss, kids. Plenty of room for everybody. Yet the birds are fighting over the feeders as if they held the last sip of sugar water on earth.

There are two males, and each has staked out a feeder. They perch on nearby branches, and when other birds approach for a drink, the males dive like Stukas and drive the others away. They seem to take great delight in it. "Boys will be boys," I say to myself.

The males head elsewhere for awhile and the females take over. Three female hummingbirds battling over one feeder, like crazed shoppers at a half-price shoe sale. The females employ the same shock tactics as the males — slashing dive, thrumming wings, high-pitched chattering. But that's not sufficient, so they resort to a more direct approach. They simply bash into each other. Remember roller derby on TV?

By late afternoon, the hummingbird squadron will tire of aerial warfare. The air will cool, the light will get softer. Three female birds will circle the same feeder in a delicate ballet, then light and drink. The males, wary of such cooperation, will look on from their perches, then cautiously join them, encouraged by the ladies' example. A spirit of peaceful coexistence will settle across my porch.

The river below the house is lively with human traffic this afternoon. Canoers, tubers, kayakers. They are not as frenzied as the hummingbirds, but they provide their own entertainment.

Two canoes drift by. Mother and small daughter in the lead, father and small son behind. Father and son are furiously working the paddles, calling out instructions to each other. "Watch that rock!" "Go left! No, right!." "Paddle on the other side!" Canoeing for these two is a project. The river is placid here, but their level of activity befits a raging section of the Colorado.

Up ahead, mother and daughter are content to slip quietly along, enjoying the river and each other's company. It's no big deal if they sideswipe a rock or bump into the bank. They talk in soft tones, watch for wildlife, experience the river. Father and son gallantly let the ladies keep the lead. Impatient, they are, but gallant. "Boys will be boys," I say to myself.

My thoughts drift to another kind of entertainment. The night before, Paulette and I enjoyed a sterling performance at the Blowing Rock Stage Company: a musical comedy, "Zombies from the Beyond." Sprightly songs, zany dialogue. Two hours of delightful weirdness. A spaceship full of alien women lands on top of a Milwaukee beauty parlor. The male characters dash about heroically, enervated by crisis and intrigue. Zombina, leader of the aliens, is unimpressed. She turns the men into zombies. The female characters keep their cool. They are the ones who ultimately vanquish Zombina and her fellow invaders, saving their men from destruction and foolishness.

I recall a piece of long-ago wisdom from my daughter Lee. She was about five at the time, and as I was tucking her into bed one night, she announced solemnly, "I know the difference between boys and girls." It was during the time when the Equal Rights Amendment was being hotly debated. And I figured that wisdom on the subject might come from any number of unexpected sources.

"What's the difference?" I asked.

"Boys are bigger," she said, "but girls are better."

The more I've thought about that over the years, the better it sounds. Go around with a tape measure and a set of scales, and you'll find that — by and large — boys are indeed bigger. And what could be better than a girl? It's one of those rare instances where logic and emotion co-exist, where generalization carries the day.

Marinating on my porch on a Sunday afternoon, contemplating hummingbirds and canoers and Zombies from the Beyond, I wonder if we shouldn't write Lee's wisdom into the Constitution. Wouldn't it be fun to watch judges try to interpret the darn thing?

There's a Riot in My Back Yard

Each Spring, around the middle to end of March, our back yard blows up. It's called forsythia, or in my wife's colloquial terminology, yellowbelles. As I look out the window of my upstairs office, the one where I do my writing, I see an explosion of yellow — the long, thin branches of the forsythia laden with blooms, rocketing skyward like a fireworks factory gone nuts. The forsythia itself is distraction enough for a fellow trying to make a living with his wits. What's worse is that the explosion is the signal for all kinds of mischief among the creatures of the back yard. It's hard to concentrate on the comparatively mundane stuff of my imagination.

The forsythia began innocently enough several years ago when Paulette brought back a few cuttings from her mother's yard in Birmingham. Paulette and her mother are forever exchanging growing things, and since the climates in Charlotte and Birmingham are similar, most of what they exchange grows. We have St. Augustine grass flourishing in our yard, a rarity in this area. A touch of Old South elegance among the pedestrian fescue. But nothing compares to the forsythia.

Paulette planted the cuttings along the back edge of a natural area near the rear of our property. Over the first summer and fall, the cuttings grew into small plants. The next spring, they shyly put forth a few blooms. And then they took off. Forsythia are like gangly teenagers, limbs flopping in all directions. Where a branch touches the ground, it takes root. And then the roots run underground and pop up yards away in the form of another bush. Soon, what began as a few cuttings became a forsythia jungle.

Once a year, the forsythia explode into a riot of yellow. The blooms last a couple of weeks. Then they wither, leaving that maze of gawky bushes. That's when the debate starts at our house about trimming the forsythia. I am no gardener, but I am convinced they would benefit greatly by being whacked about the head and shoulders. But two things prevent the kind of drastic pruning I recommend. Firstly, Paulette won't allow it. Oh, she'll take a nip here and a tuck there, but you can see that it wounds her deeply to do even that. Secondly, as for me, I'm afraid to venture into the thicket. I may never be seen again.

So, the forsythia remain. I resign myself to a couple of weeks of awed viewing from the office window. And I catalog what else is going on in the back yard — set in motion, perhaps, by the pyrotechnics.

Most of the activity is around the bird houses. We have several and they attract a variety of tenants. Chickadees in the little gabled affair under the photinia. Nuthatches in the house next to the patio that's decorated to resemble a red barn. Finches in the A-frame next to the bird bath. All manner of hanky-panky is going on up in the trees, and those eggs have to go somewhere. So couples are checking out the available properties, staking their claims, and beginning the furious job of interior decorating.

All of this is fascinating to watch, even more so because of our anticipation of Act Two: hatching the young'uns and feeding their insatiable appetites; and Act Three: babes leaving the nest.

Last year, we witnessed the Great Flight from the red barn in all its drama. It began early on a Saturday morning, and Paulette and I stood at an upstairs window and took it all in. One by one, the babies stuck their heads out, sniffed the air, then climbed out on the perch and, with a little coaxing from their parents, fluttered away. All except for the last little guy. He had to be pulled kicking and screaming out of the house, and when he got on the perch, he froze there, chirping his head off. Mom tried coaxing. No luck. She tried luring Junior with a morsel. Naaaahhh. So, her patience exhausted, she simply kicked him off. He fell like a rock into the azalea bush at the base of the bird house and thrashed about there for a good ten minutes. Paulette and I feared the worst from neighborhood cats. But finally, with parents shouting encouragement, Junior struggled to the uppermost branch of the azalea and, with a deep breath, took flight. It was an Academy Award performance.

That's the kind of entertainment going on in our back yard each spring. All of it, against the passionate backdrop of exploding forsythia. What the heck, I say, let 'em grow. And what the heck, I'll get the writing done next week.

Hippos, Weavers, and Brown Honey Guides

I figure a man of my age can always learn something. I welcome opportunities to expand the horizons of my knowledge, often at times and in ways I scarcely suspect.

I went to Africa awhile back, and I learned a good deal while I was there. Some of what I learned is useful. For instance, you don't stand too close to a body of water in which you can't see the bottom. Crocodiles frequent such places, and they can leap out and drag you beneath the lily pads before you can say "Uh-oh." But such things are basics of survival in the bush. There are other lessons from nature that are much more subtle and intriguing. These are things I learned from one old hippo and two birds.

The Hippo

We started to ford the Luangwa River one day in our Land Cruiser to find a lone hippopotamus standing in the middle of the river, right where we needed to drive. He was, as the girls like to say, a "hunk" — at least as big as our truck and equipped with a much better four-wheel drive. Needless to say, we waited while the hippo took his time meandering downstream a ways, bellowing and shaking his head at us all the while. He seemed to be an altogether ill-tempered fellow. A hippo curmudgeon. We were not at all surprised to learn from our guide that it had mostly to do with sex.

Our hippo was an old, ostracized male. At one time not long ago he had been the head honcho in his hippo pod, doted on by his extensive harem of ladies, idolized by the children, feared by the younger males. But, as baseball great Satchell Paige used to say, "Don't look back, something might be gaining on you." In this case, it was one of the young males who grew to prodigious size and maturity and decided it was time to take on the big guy. The youngster threw down the challenge and they had it out at midstream. These fights are brutal, often to the death. In this case, the old fellow lost but survived. And thus became an outcast.

Nature has programmed all this into the hippo world. The dominant male gets to have all the love affairs in his pod, to father all the children. After about three years of this exquisite experience, his daughters are growing into sexual maturity. And the old fellow is beginning to wear out. So it's time for a young male to challenge his dominance and send him to the showers, lest the old guy start breeding with his own offspring. It keeps the bloodline fresh, you see. But it's clearly tough on the vanquished fellow, who grumbles and snorts and appears thoroughly miserable, deprived as he is of the delights of hippo flesh.

What did I learn from all this? Well, I suppose, that hippos don't grow old gracefully and are a pain in the rear in retirement. I hope to do better.

The Weaver

There are several species of weaver birds, but they share a common trait: the males of the species are long-suffering chumps.

Weavers build attractive and elaborate nests in bushes and trees — whole colonies of nests that look like Japanese lanterns hung from the branches. The male weaver is the builder, working under his wife's instruction. She shows him where to build a nest and he scurries about getting the job done. Then she inspects it, shakes her head, and says, "Nope." So he builds another one. And another. Eventually, she will pronounce one of his structures satisfactory and will settle in to have the babies.

Again, nature has hard-wired this into weaver instinct. All of those empty nests are decoys. Lady weavers — wise and perceptive creatures that they are — are simply trying to outwit predators. The more empty nests, the less likelihood the real one will get raided. Do the male weavers know this? Obviously not, or they would rebel. What I learned from the weavers is, sometimes men are better off ignorant.

The Brown Honey Guide

When you hike through the bush, you will

often gain the company of a small brown bird that will chatter hysterically as it flits from bush to tree. Most hikers ignore the honey guide, but if you were to follow him, he would lead you to a honey-filled beehive, in hopes of sharing the spoils. You're welcome to the honey. He wants the beeswax. The honey guide is so busy trying to guide, he doesn't have time to build nests. His wife lays eggs in the nests of other birds.

What did I learn from the brown honey guide? That he's smarter than the weaver and not as hen-pecked.

I'm still grieving for that old hippo and the poor dumb male weaver bird. We guys have it tough, don't we.

A World Held Together by Grandparents

Our friends are brand-new first-time grandparents, and there is a special glow about them that warms the heart. They've been to Florida, where the blessed event took place, and they are back now with photos of themselves with their handsome, strapping grandson. In the pictures, the grandparents are grinning like folks who've just discovered the fountain of youth. The kid seems a little bored with the whole thing. *So this is what it's like out here. What's for dinner? Same old stuff?* The grandparents have, indeed, found something — that special joy of being, well, grandparents. It's parenthood once removed, without most of the muss and fuss — childbirth without labor or breastfeeding; no braces or adolescent angst or college tuitions to worry about. Spoil 'em and send 'em home.

Grandparents, it goes without saying, hold a special place in our lives. They're a source of wisdom, a vital link in the chain of knowledge that can help unravel some of the mysteries of parenting. To a grandchild, they're the folks who can praise without reservation and overlook all shortcomings. Grandparents can magnify even the most modest accomplishments and talents until the child becomes a paragon of genius and beauty. Occasionally, the kid even starts believing all that stuff and lives up to it.

I started thinking about grandparents when I read a story about elephants in Africa. In many areas, game poachers have wiped out much of the elephant population. The first elephants they go after are, of course, the biggest — the old bulls and the matriarchs, the ones with the longest tusks and the most meat. Killing an old elephant means destroying generations of wisdom — the knowledge of what it means to be an adult, how you go about being a parent. The result is that younger elephants, deprived of the example of the elders, are poor parents. Many of their young die from neglect, compounding tragedy with tragedy.

Thank goodness, we humans don't have to contend with poachers. Our dilemma is much more subtle — parents and grandparents playing a delicate game in which wisdom is passed on by the older generation without the younger surrendering its parental independence. Young parents ought to have room to make mistakes. Goodness knows, *their* parents did. But, they did some things right, too.

I think grandparenting has changed a good deal in the past fifty years because of the way America has changed. I thought about that when I got behind a car with Colorado license plates, a silver-haired couple in the front seat, a sticker on the rear bumper that read, "It's Great To Be Grandparents." The picture was obvious: some folks who had driven cross-country for a visit with children and grandchildren here in the Carolinas. It's a common occurrence, especially in a city like Charlotte where most of us are from somewhere else. We've left parents and grandparents behind in Georgia or Pennsylvania or Colorado and we're busy here with our careers and our family-raising.

Still, we have a sense of where we came from, of time and place and extended family. That's important, because we're sort of adrift if we don't have a history and some connections. And often, it's the grandparents who keep those connections alive. We don't have time to get back to Georgia or Pennsylvania or Colorado very often, so the grandparents do the traveling — bringing their love and wisdom with them and adding an essential texture to our lives. Planes, trains and automobiles bridge the time and space between generations and let our young know what it means to be part of that on-flowing stream that is a family in its broadest sense.

We've always been a nation on the move. If that weren't the case, we would never have settled this immense country. We were always willing to pull up stakes and see what kind of green pasture we could find just over the next hill. But we're settlers, too. We put down roots and put great stock in having our kin in close proximity. Junior lived right down the hollow from Mama and Daddy, and on Sunday afternoon, the entire caterwauling clan of parents and grandparents, aunts and uncles and cousins gathered at Big Mama and Big Daddy's house, the old home place, to tell some truths and lies and perpetuate the family's myths and legends.

It still happens that way for some folks. But for many, a great change came about in the midpoint of this century when the Depression and World War Two uprooted and scattered us, and then corporate America took over. Moving is a fact of life for many families. If you're not careful, you can lose touch with that essential part of yourself that you call your history, that place where the wisdom is. Grandparents, bless their souls, are perhaps our best defense against that.

Now that Paulette and I are grandparents, we keep our bags packed, ready at a moment's notice or even a whim to jet off to Colorado where we have grandparent work to do. We're portable. We may even have a little wisdom to share. On request, of course.

My Friend Delbert Earle

Famous for Fifteen Minutes

My friend Delbert Earle called to say that he's thinking about changing jobs. He's filing an application with this company he's interested in, and wanted to know if he could list me as a reference.

"Of course," I said. "I'll give you my highest recommendation. I'll lie or tell the truth, whichever will do you the most good."

"You know," said Delbert Earle, "I wouldn't have to go through all this — the application and the references — if I were famous. They'd just call and say, 'Delbert Earle, we need a famous guy like you.'"

"But you *are* famous," I protested. "Your name appears frequently in my writings."

"But not my picture," said Delbert Earle. "You're not famous until people know what you look like."

It is an old and shopworn issue between us. For some years now, first on television and then in the local newspaper, I have been writing about my friend Delbert Earle. I know no other person on earth who provides such a wealth of material on the vagaries of modern life and human nature. Every one of us knows someone like Delbert Earle. Some of us *are* Delbert Earle. He and his wife and his boy Elrod and his Great Uncle Orester are great grist for a writer, and I faithfully record their human comedy. You'd think they would all stop speaking to me after some of the things I tell about them. But no, they are enamored of the idea of fame. They're sort of a local version of the kind of folks who get on TV talk shows and reveal things you'd just as soon they had kept to themselves. Delbert Earle and his kin aren't kinky, but they are, shall we say, interesting.

But back to the photograph business. Over the years, Delbert Earle has sent me several pictures of himself. One was what's commonly called in the trade a "mug shot." Delbert Earle went to a studio that specializes in glamour photos. Their clientele is almost exclusively female, but Delbert Earle insisted on having his picture taken there. So they dressed him in a Nehru jacket and an ascot and poofed up his hair. The result was a bit like Liberace on vacation. He even autographed the photo: "To Bob with admiration and affection from his loyal friend Delbert Earle." Out of respect for Delbert Earle's image, I did not publish it.

There have been others, usually more candid shots. One shows Delbert Earle mowing the grass while his boy Elrod looks on from the front stoop. Another shows Delbert Earle sitting patiently on a bench outside a department store at the mall while his wife shops inside. Another has him delivering a pot of his wife's famous chicken soup to a sick neighbor. All of those photos reside in a special file in my office. It is enough, I think, to tell you that Delbert Earle does all those things, and that you might think well of him because of it.

Delbert Earle continues to drop not-so-subtle hints about photographs, and I continue to tell him that fame is a double-edged sword. There is a certain safety in anonymity. I can speak first-hand of that, because I have become a little more anonymous since I stopped appearing on TV. Occasionally, someone will ask, "Didn't you use to be Bob Inman?" Sometimes I admit to it. Sometimes not.

Fame, I tell Delbert Earle, can be the ruination of good people. I remind him of what happened to his Great Uncle Orester's wife. She makes some of the best peanut butter spice cake you can imagine from a secret family recipe. The neighbors in their rural community raved so about her talent that she and Orester got the bright idea of offering cakes for sale at the store just down the road from their house. They sold like crazy. Orester's wife couldn't bake them fast enough. Her fame, modest though it was, spread.

The downfall came when Orester got the bright idea of telling the local newspaper about his wife's burgeoning home business. They sent a reporter and photographer to her kitchen and did a full-page spread. Friends and neighbors sent clippings. Orester's wife, heady with her newfound fame, doubled her prices. The neighbors all got mad and started boycotting the store. She folded the business and has just now, with the help of generous gifts of spice cake, gotten back in the good graces of folks in the area.

One fellow said that in our modern time, each one of us will be famous for 15 minutes. Delbert Earle says he's still waiting for his. He dreams of stepping out of a private jet or a stretch limousine, waving to an adoring crowd, signing autographs, being interviewed by Dan Rather.

I tell him it's much better to be a man of mystery. And if he's determined to get his picture in the paper, he can wait until his obituary appears. I suggest he insist on using the photo with the poofed-up hairdo. We'll all have a good chuckle and he won't have to hear it.

What's Spring?
Love and Open Windows

Ah, spring. And love is in full bloom at my friend Delbert Earle's house — mushy, sappy, breathaking love. His boy Elrod is the victim. Delbert Earle, comfortable in the calmer, more comfortable love of a long and happy marriage, is content to watch and remember.

Every morning these days, Elrod drifts down to breakfast on a cloud of Aramis after-shave — scrubbed, combed and moon-eyed. By breakfast, Elrod and his girlfriend have talked at least three times by telephone. Delbert Earle wonders what people say to each other that early in the morning. He and his wife, lovers though they may be, are barely civil before eight.

Once at the breakfast table, Elrod will stare at his grapefruit and oatmeal for awhile, sigh deeply, and get up from the table. He will go back upstairs, brush his teeth for the fourth time, dab on a little more Aramis and some Clearasil, and depart the house.

Soon, Elrod and his girlfriend will be sitting so close in the front seat of Elrod's Trans-Am that you couldn't pass a piece of plastic wrap between them. His Aramis mingling with her Enjoli, the car vibrating with the thunder of a guitar-smashing rock band on the CD player. *Oooga-chukka, oooga-chukka.*

My friend Delbert Earle is occasionally tempted to make wisecracks. But then he remembers another boy and girl on another spring morning, driving to school in a green '53 Chevy, his Aqua Velva mingled with her White Shoulders, every sense alive and bursting, the air sweet with the sound of the Drifters on the dashboard radio. *Shoo-boobey-do-WAH.*

Only the singers have changed, Delbert Earle says. Love and lyrics are ageless.

Later in the day, while Delbert Earle is at work, he will think again of love and how it can get you in hot water. He will remember Miz Pirtley. She was his senior English teacher and her favorite saying was, "Delbert Earle, if you ever quit acting the fool, you might amount to something."

Delbert Earle thought he was quite the dude in the spring of his senior year. He was playing shortstop on the baseball team, going steady with a girl so cute he blushed every time he thought of her, and about to graduate. Well, hoping to graduate.

Delbert Earle was the class cut-up, always the center of attention, and something of a practical jokester. Anytime Miz Pirtley found something in her desk drawer that wasn't supposed to be there, she knew exactly where it came from. And she found a good many strange things in her desk drawer the spring of Delbert Earle's senior year. But she exacted a sweet revenge.

One warm afternoon, Delbert Earle was standing on top of a desk in study hall, leaning out the open window, talking to his girlfriend. Miz Pirtley passed by in the hall, took in the scene, and moved faster than anybody had ever seen her move before. She grabbed Delbert Earle by the ankles, gave a mighty shove, and tossed him clean out the window into a nandina bush. Then Miz Pirtley climbed up on the desk and smiled out the window at Delbert Earle.

"What did you go and do that for?" he yelped, his pride more wounded than his person.

"Delbert Earle," she said sweetly, "I was just acting the fool, and it was too good an opportunity to pass up."

Well, Delbert Earle turned out all right. He's got a good job and a nice family now, pays his taxes and never misses voting in an election. He's acted the fool a number of times in his life (haven't we all?), but a few times he started to and didn't, and it was the memory of Miz Pirtley that dissuaded him. The next time he passes the school, he intends to drop in and thank Miz Pirtley for setting him on the straight and narrow. But he plans to stay clear of the windows.

For the moment, Delbert Earle is content to watch his boy Elrod play the fool. Elrod is not the class clown that Delbert Earle was in his teenage years. As far as any of us know, he's never been tossed out a window by Miz Pirtley or anyone else. But this young lady who sits so close to him in the front seat of the Trans-Am, enveloped in a cloud of Enjoli and exquisite sweetness, has turned a strapping boy into silly putty. He makes foolish faces and utters foolish nonsense.

Ah, to be a fool in love. There's nothing quite so ridiculously wonderful. Delbert Earle remembers it well. He tells me he plans to stop on the way home from work one day this week and purchase flowers and champagne. Once home, he will woo and coo and act the fool. After all, it's spring.

February: A Month We Can Do Without

E very time a new year dawns, I start giving some thought to banning February.

I wish I could claim credit for the idea, but credit belongs to my friend Delbert Earle, who is capable of occasional leaps of imaginative brilliance. Watching Delbert Earle's mind at work is similar to that old definition of flying: hours of sheer boredom interspersed with moments of stark terror. Well, Delbert Earle had one of those moments awhile back and he called me promptly on the telephone. "Hey!" he yelled. That's always the way he starts his conversations. "Hey! Don't you think we oughta do away with February?"

I've learned that the best thing to do when this sort of thing happens is to just agree with Delbert Earle and let him ramble on about whatever cockeyed idea he has come up with at the moment. Except this time, it was not cockeyed at all. I instantly recognized a stroke of genius. I let him ramble on, as always, but I knew that the man was onto something.

Delbert Earle's call came after a spell of particularly mild Winter weather, and it was his opinion that such occurrences lull us into a false sense of security. Get a few pleasant days in January, and people begin to delude themselves into thinking that Winter is not so bad after all, and may in fact just about be over. Birds fly north, we wash our cars, and clothing stores put bikini-clad mannequins in their windows. Delbert Earle said when that happens, we're being set up.

Then comes stark reality. February hits and along with it, the dismal drearies: snow and ice, gloom and angst, public unrest and domestic discontent. We're reminded that February is the most abominable month on the calendar. The only thing that redeems February is Valentine's Day, and even that can be dicey if you forget the card and the candy.

Of course, lots of folks like basketball on TV in February. But lots of others are incensed when the prime time game pre-empts some favorite sitcom or cops and robbers show. Each home probably has one of each. As I say, domestic discontent.

Delbert Earle says it's especially bad at his house in February. Old Shep holes up under the house with his head between his paws, refusing to come out even for the garbage truck. His boy Elrod inevitably breaks up with his girlfriend during the month and spends hours in his room playing mournful old Everly Brothers records. *Teen angel, teen angel, woooooooahhhhhh.* And Delbert Earle's wife has that wild look in her eyes that says, "Shop or die."

Delbert Earle says some terrible things have happened to other members of his family in Februarys past. It was in February that his Great Uncle Orester got involved in the futures market. Futures, as wily investors know, amount to buying something that doesn't exist. And Orester bought pomegranates. He bought them from Happy Otto, who showed up at Orester's door one dismal February morning, selling vinyl siding, encyclopedias, and futures. He convinced Orester that pomegranates were the ticket to quick riches, and since Orester had rather be rich quicker than slower, he bit. Or bought.

Well, about the time the pomegranate harvest came in, the bottom dropped out of the market. Growers couldn't even sell them to the government because Congress had just done away with the pomegranate support program. Orester wondered what was going to happen to all those newly-harvested but unsold pomegranates. More importantly, he wondered what was going to happen to his riches. Then one day he found out. A big truck pulled up and dumped three tons of pomegranates into Orester's front yard, right between the mimosa tree and the stoop. Delbert Earle is charitable with his relatives. He doesn't believe Orester was dumb or naïve, just that his judgment was clouded by February.

So, Delbert Earle believes he is onto something when he proposes banning February. The first year he thought of it, he promptly dashed off a letter to the White House, proposing an emergency international summit. He said it has to be a global thing. It wouldn't do for some countries to have February and others not. He would, however, make an exception for Iraq. He thinks February does just fine there. Whenever the summit is eventually held, Delbert Earle is prepared to testify to the assembled world leaders and he is looking for more anecdotal evidence to bolster his case. Things like Orester's pomegranate debacle.

Each year, Delbert Earle calls me in mid-January in a panic, realizing that time is of the essence. In a few more days it will be too late and our only recourse will be to hunker down and endure another February. Each January he says he doesn't think he's man enough to go through that again.

I will keep you informed of Delbert Earle's progress, if any. He is hopeful, as am I. If, some year, you pick up your local paper in Feburary and see that it's dated March, you'll know he succeeded. Until then, he may show up at your house with a petition. Please sign.

Wanted: Goblin or Some Facsimile

I f you ever happen to run into my friend Delbert Earle around Halloween, you'll find him on his annual quest for the meaning of the word "goblin." It has become an important part of our Halloween vocabulary, something we toss around as if we really knew what it meant. But Delbert Earle says if you try to pin down your average person on exactly what a goblin is, you're likely to get a lot of hemming and hawing.

The dictionary says a goblin is a "grotesque, elfin creature of folklore, thought to work mischief or evil." But Delbert Earle says that sounds a little too much like his mother-in-law. He's looking for something a bit more specific, and has been, in fact, since childhood.

Delbert Earle says when he was seven, he announced to his big sister Imogene that he wanted to be a wooly booger for Halloween. Delbert Earle didn't know any more about wooly boogers than he did goblins, but he had it in his mind that anything with a name like "wooly booger" must be a fearsome creature. And at seven, Delbert Earle wanted more than anything in the world to be fearsome. So Imogene used her imagination. She made him a coat out of a burlap sack and a hat out of a gourd. She covered the whole business with Spanish moss, and then for good measure, spray-painted it purple and green. From all accounts, Delbert Earle looked like something that had emerged at midnight from your local waste treatment plant.

Thusly attired as a fearsome wooly booger, Delbert Earle went out trick-or-treating. He would go up to a house and knock on the door and a lady would come to the door and either scream or laugh. Then when she recovered, she'd invariably say, "Why here's a cute little goblin."

Delbert Earle would get hopping mad. "Naw lady," he would snort fearsomely, "I ain't no goblin, I'm a wooly booger."

"Well, do you want some candy?" the lady would ask.

"Naw, I don't want nothing from nobody that don't know a wooly booger from a goblin." And he would stalk off.

After about an hour of this, Delbert Earle gave up and went home, his trick-or-treat sack empty and his fearsomeness in disarray. That was, in fact, the last year Delbert Earle went trick-or-treating on Halloween. After that, he just stayed home and made faces at himself in the mirror.

Ever since, Delbert Earle has been trying to pin down this business of goblins. He recently enlisted me in his search. And together, we've gotten absolutely nowhere. Folks just don't seem to know much about goblins, no matter how freely they use the word. We conducted an informal poll down at Cheap Ernie's Pool Hall and

Microbrewery, but none of the guys had a clue. Sure, they've heard the word, but ask for details and you get blank looks. Now ghosts, they know. Ghosts wear sheets, moan a lot, and disappear through the wall. Some of the guys down at Cheap Ernie's could probably qualify as ghosts. But there's not a goblin expert in the bunch.

Last Halloween, Delbert Earle hit upon the idea of bringing Old Shep the Wonder Dog into the business. He rummaged through a trunk and found the old burlap sack and gourd from his long-ago wooly booger costume. His uncle Fitzwaller in Louisiana sent a fresh supply of Spanish moss. Delbert Earle decked out Old Shep in the get-up, applied purple and green spray paint, and put Old Shep out on the front porch with a sign that read, "Goblin Dog." He figured he would at least get some opinions from the kids that came by trick-or-treating.

The problem was, Old Shep got it into his mind that he was fearsome. He's normally the most gentle and lovable of animals, but wearing that get-up, his personality changed. He growled and snarled and scared all the trick-or-treaters away. Even the next day when Delbert Earle re-moved the costume, Old Shep remained fearsome. Neighbors began to complain about his rude and obnoxious behavior. The postmaster called and said, "Delbert Earle, if you don't do something about Old Shep, you're gonna lose home deliv-ery." It took six weeks of watching soap operas for Old Shep to return to normal.

So, that didn't work. Halloween comes and goes and we still don't know what a goblin is. If we don't get some reliable information between now and next Halloween, I'm afraid of what Delbert Earle may try. He's written to Uncle Fitzwaller in

Louisiana for more Spanish moss, and he's mentioned to his mother-in-law that he has an idea about her Halloween costume. Given the experience with Old Shep, I hate to think what could happen.

Now I Know Where My Belly-Button Went

My friend Delbert Earle and I were so happy to read in the newspaper that the universe is expanding.

In case you missed the story, let us bring you up to speed. Scientists have come up with startling new findings about the cosmos. Until now, most agreed with the notion that the universe is in a sort of balance, neither contracting nor expanding. But now, using new technology, they've found what they describe as a "mysterious force" that seems to be tugging at the universe and counteracting the pull of gravity. Stars and galaxies, they say, are flying apart at an ever-increasing rate.

There is considerable debate about this new idea, and it will keep the astronomers and physicists and cosmologists happily busy for years trying to prove or disprove each other. For Delbert Earle and me — well, we're ready to accept the new theory as hard fact. It explains a lot.

Finally, we know what happens to things we lose. And don't we lose a lot of things? The car keys, single socks, kids' jackets, false teeth, the photo negatives from Aunt Tillie's 94th birthday party. Where do they go? They fall through the cracks formed by the expanding universe. The whole business must work something like an accordion, contracting and expanding, because lost items occasionally pop up. But many of them are gone forever, into some sort of nether-dimension, populated by the ghosts of Sir Isaac Newton and Albert Einstein. It probably drives Ike and Al crazy, all those odd socks and car keys floating around.

Delbert Earle says he tried to touch his toes the other day, but couldn't. He is happy to discover that the problem is not his affinity for Little Debbie cakes, it's the expanding universe. The thing is, it's farther to his toes than it used to be. The same principle applies to his morning commute to work. He says it takes him longer to get there than it used to. The roads are expanding, but only lengthwise. If they would expand sideways, we could get more cars on them. But that's not how the law of the expanding universe works.

It also explains why athletes are so much bigger these days. Several eons ago, I played high school football as a 135-pound defensive end. Today, a 135-pound high school football player is on a suicide mission. Even at that level, the athletes are behemoths. Your favorite college or pro team has several players the size of moving vans. Sumo wrestlers are no longer oddities. And whenever a community talks about building a new gymnasium, it must consider a higher roof so the basketball players won't bump their heads. It's all due to the expanding universe.

I don't want to stretch the point beyond credulity, but the notion of an ever-expanding universe may lie at the bottom of all sorts of puzzles:

why it takes Congress all year to do its work when the Honorables used to wrap it up in a few weeks and go home; why the shampoo you buy at the drugstore gives you 25% more absolutely free; and why we aren't as envious of Texas as we used to be.

If all this makes you raise your eyebrows in disbelief, listen to Robert Kirshner of the Harvard-Smithsonian Center for Astrophysics, commenting on the expanding-universe theory: "This is nutty sounding," he says, "but it's the simplest explanation for the data we've got." As we are aware, people from Harvard and the Smithsonian always know what they're talking about.

I've always been partial to innovative and even oddball scientific theories. In a book I once wrote, an elderly character tells his grandson how submarines work: when the crew wants the sub to descend, they all sit down; when they want it to rise, they all stand up. The grandson never knew when to believe the old man, but the idea was great fun. My friend Delbert Earle, who thinks I'm a little oddball on many counts, thought the submarine idea was one of the most logical things I've ever put in a book. And he believes the Theory of the Expanding Universe is worth a great deal of further study by the kind of folks you find at Harvard and the Smithsonian. Meantime, he plans to make full use of it around the house. As in:

Delbert Earle's wife: "Delbert Earle, did you take out the garbage like I told you to?"

Delbert Earle: "No ma'am."

Delbert Earle's wife: "Why not?"

Delbert Earle: "It's the expanding universe."

Delbert Earle's wife: "Say what?"

Delbert Earle: "The universe is getting bigger all the time. Things fall through the cracks.

Even thoughts."

Delbert Earle's wife: "You mean, there's more space between your ears than there used to be?"

Delbert Earle: "Well..."

The Soul of a Poet and a Good Shovel

Spring always puts my friend Delbert Earle in a strange frame of mind. His heart is filled with love, but he begins to feel twinges in the small of his back — his lumbago sending warning signals to the rest of his body.

It generally starts around Valentine's Day. It's hard not to have a heart filled with love on Valentine's Day. Delbert Earle cherishes the company and affection of the good woman he was fortunate enough to marry some years ago. He brings flowers and candy. He wanders about the house emoting lines from Browning:

How do I love thee?
Let me count the ways.

He remembers the first time he heard those lines, in a high school English class on a Spring afternoon with the world bursting outside and his heart aglow with unrequited love for Myrtle Spence, who sat two rows over near the pencil sharpener. Delbert Earle went through a number of pencils that Spring, just to get a whiff of Myrtle's perfume. When the English teacher called Myrtle to the front of the room and had her read aloud the words of Elizabeth Barrett Browning, Delbert Earle had to lay his head down on his desk for fear of fainting dead away.

After high school, Myrtle Spence married an insurance salesman and moved to Boise, Idaho. When she turned up at a high school reunion a couple of years ago, she had, alas, shed much of her youthful charm and grace. Delbert Earle realized that it was not so much Myrtle Spence that he was in love with back there in that English class, it was the very idea of love. Delbert Earle was proud to introduce Myrtle to his good wife, who has stuck with him through thick and thin, through the passage of years in which he has shed much of his own youthful charm and grace.

Delbert Earle thinks now of Boise, Idaho in the dead of Winter and shivers, thankful for Spring in the South and the love of his good woman. "My love is like a red, red rose," he warbles. And then he shivers again, thinking that if it is nearly Spring, it is nearly Spring Transplanting Time.

Delbert Earle's wife is a right fair amateur gardener. She has a way with annuals and perennials, shrubs and flowers. She also has a way with Delbert Earle, who does the grunt work of gardening about her yard. His wife likes to don floppy hat, gardening smock, and gloves and flit about the yard snipping and plucking. And giving directions to Delbert Earle, who lifts and totes, digs and covers up. His wife is forever bringing home new plantings from the nursery and moving those she already has.

Delbert Earle knows it is almost Spring when his wife looks out the kitchen window at the back yard and says, "I think the mahonia would look better over yonder." He knows that his wife has already rearranged the yard in her mind. Now it only remains for Delbert Earle to do the work. He braces himself for a frantic flurry of activity, because as any good gardener knows, transplanting must be done before Spring growth bursts forth. Ah love, ah lumbago.

Delbert Earle's only consolation is that the situation will be even more complicated over at his great-uncle Orester's house. Orester will again hire Delbert Earle's boy Elrod to help him in the yard. It is a strange alliance, born of necessity. Orester himself is a man of the soil, raised on a farm by a family of optimists who always thought kudzu would some day be a cash crop. Elrod simply needs the money.

The work at Orester's house always begins on an afternoon when the weather is unseasonably warm and full of the promise of impending Spring. Elrod will take his boom box to the job site and turn it on at its usual explosive volume. He will hang his shirt on a limb and proceed to dig a little bitty hole to receive a dwarf holly that is being moved across the yard.

Orester will approach, survey the hole, and say to Elrod, "Never dig a nickel hole for a 25-cent plant."

"What?" Elrod will yell, "I can't hear you."

Orester will reach over, turn off the boom box, and repeat his instructions. An hour later, hands blistered and eyes bloodshot, Elrod will finally have the hole big enough to suit Orester. But while he digs, he will turn the boom box back on and let it blast away.

That's the way it invariably goes at Orester's house when it's Spring Transplanting Time. The two generations learn a great deal from each other. With each passing year, Elrod digs bigger and better holes. And Orester develops a reluctant but passable tolerance for boogie music. They have gotten to the point where they converse knowledgeably on peat humus and potash and on the relative merits of Hank Williams, Junior and his late lamented daddy. There is, as Delbert Earle puts it, more than one kind of transplanting going on at Orester's.

At his own place, Delbert Earle will survey the back yard, give his wife a Valentine's Day hug and kiss, and go upstairs to take two aspirin.

High Technology and Dinosaur Eggs

My friend Delbert Earle says he was mighty glad to read in the paper about the dinosaur eggs.

Scientists have long been under the impression that the dinosaurs were wiped out sixty-five million years ago when a giant meteor hit the earth and created a cloud of dust so thick it blotted out the sun. But now, a fellow in China says he has found some fossilized dinosaur eggs that are much younger, proving that dinosaurs lived long after they were supposedly extinct. Delbert Earle is under the impression, in fact, that dinosaurs are still living. And he's one of them.

Delbert Earle and I got into this deep paleontological discussion when I was over at his place and found him talking to his computer. He was trying to email a photograph of his family reunion to an old maid sister in Rock Hill, South Carolina, and was not having much luck. "Shoot, Delbert Earle," I said, "Rock Hill isn't all that far from your house. Why don't you just take the picture over there." But to my good friend, it was the principle of the thing. His wife went and bought this computer so they could email things to their far-flung relatives (some live even farther away than Rock Hill) and he was trying manfully to make it work. He was muttering things to his computer that I wouldn't repeat in polite company. It was his good wife who opined that he is a technological dinosaur, and Delbert Earle agreed.

I opined that Delbert Earle was going about things all wrong. Not that I know all that much about computers, mind you, but I learned a lesson some years ago about how to treat inanimate objects: that is, you talk to the object *before* the fact, not after.

I learned this from a politician friend named Pete who was a poor but enthusiastic golfer. He was a legislator, a master of compromise, and he approached golf the same way he did his legislative duties. My friend Pete would step up to the tee and address his ball directly. "Now ball," he would say, "we can work out a deal here. What I need is about two-hundred yards, just enough to get past the dogleg. And if you find it in your capacity to do so, I would appreciate your avoiding the trap on the right." Then Pete would hit the ball. Sometimes it did what he asked. Pete opined that all this business of keeping your head down and your elbow straight and spending lots of money on a Big Bertha driver was a lot of baloney. It was, to his mind, all a matter of persuasion.

I admit that my friend Pete's technique worked better for him than for me, at least on the golf course. I gave up golf for Lent some years ago, having tried Pete's way and failed. But I have found it useful in other venues. "Lawnmower," I will say, "there's rain in the forecast for the afternoon, so if we can get our work done in the next couple of hours, it would keep both of us from getting wet. I'd appreciate your starting on the first pull, or at least no later than the twentieth." Sometimes the lawnmower will respond. "Computer," I will say, "I have to get this letter of supplication written to the IRS by five o'clock, and since it is three now, I would appreciate your not eating what I type and having it disappear into some yawning black hole of cyberspace." Sometimes the computer will do what I ask.

Delbert Earle is skeptical. He has never had much luck with high-tech — lawnmowers, computers, golf balls, or any such. He is still a bit gun-shy after the beeper debacle.

Some time ago, he was given a beeper at work so his boss could keep up with him. Delbert Earle was right proud of his beeper because it showed he was indispensable. He showed it to his wife that night and gave her the number for his beeper in case she needed him in an emergency. The next day, Delbert Earle was in a meeting at work when his beeper went, "Beep. Beep. Delbert Earle, pick up some bread and prune juice on your way home." He was right embarrassed and told his wife not to call him anymore on his beeper except in dire emergency, which did not include bread and prune juice.

That night, when he was sound asleep, the beeper went off on his bedside table. "Beep. Beep. Delbert Earle, call your office." He rushed to the phone and called the office, but of course there wasn't anybody there. He figured it was just some of the guys having fun down at the all night juke-joint.

But then he began to get really strange stuff on his beeper. "Beep. Beep. Doctor forty-nine to surgery." Or "Beep. Beep. Breaker one-nine. This is the old Fuzzbuster, good buddy. Got your ears on?" He began to pick up snippets of a radio show where a woman gives sex advice, some garbled stuff that sounded like transmissions from the space shuttle, even a guy singing "O Sole Mio" off-key with an electric razor going in the background. It began to give Delbert Earle the willies and he turned in his beeper.

He's having the same kind of dilemma with his new computer, and he's convinced himself that he'll never be modern. When I consider Delbert Earle, I remember the woman in the Brother Dave Gardner comedy routine who says to her son, "James Louis, you put down that wheelbarrow. You don't know nothing about machinery."

Like that dinosaur in China, when it comes to high-tech, Delbert Earle just lays eggs.

In Defense of Bad Habits

When the end of the year approaches, it's not only time to celebrate the joyous holiday season, it's time to pay some attention to our New Year's Resolutions. My friend Delbert Earle says his only resolution for the coming year is to cultivate some bad habits.

Delbert Earle is a generally good guy and solid citizen. He votes, pays his taxes, goes to PTA meetings, works hard, loves his family, and only occasionally tailgates. And all that solid goodness is beginning to worry him a little.

It started a couple of months ago when Delbert Earle read what Mark Twain had to say about bad habits. Twain was all for them. He smoked, cussed, and frequently told lies in print. He was cantankerous and careless with money and relished the company of disreputable characters. Twain's view was that a fellow needed a good stock of bad habits so he would always have something to give up if the need arose. He was especially fond of tobacco. Big, smelly cigars. Twain used to say, "I can give up smoking any time I want to. I've done it a thousand times."

Twain told the story of a lady who went to her physician, feeling poorly in a rather vague way. The doctor examined her thoroughly, but could find no specific ailment. The only thing he could suggest was that she give up something — tobacco, fermented spirits, late hours, the like. The problem was, she didn't have a single bad habit. The doctor shook his head and sent her home, and soon thereafter she passed away. She was, Twain said, like a sinking ship with no ballast to throw overboard. Twain himself never had that problem, and recommended that others follow his example.

Now, Delbert Earle knows that he treads on treacherous ground when he advocates the adoption of bad habits. And he wants to make it clear that he recommends nothing illegal, blatantly immoral, or particularly fattening. He goes further to point out that it's not the habit itself that's important, it's what you do with it.

Delbert Earle gives the example of a certain Royal Marriage, the messy dissolution of which occupied reams of newsprint and hours of broadcast time a few years back. Delbert Earle has it on good authority that the first crack in the facade of said Royal Marriage was over the subject of underwear.

It seems, according to Delbert Earle's sources, that the Prince was negligent about picking up his underwear. The Princess would come in from an arduous day of cutting ribbons and kissing babies to find the Prince's underwear on the floor. "Pick up your underwear," she would demand. And the Prince would call in his valet, personal secretary and assorted footmen to do the job. He was, to put it plainly, rather blithe about the business. "No, no, no!" says Delbert Earle. The proper procedure here is to admit the bad habit and take *personal* pains to rectify the situation, at least temporarily. *Mea culpa, mea maxima culpa.* Delbert Earle believes that with the proper attitude, a bad habit such as leaving underwear on the floor can be used over and over to good effect, on each occasion acknowledging one's shortcomings and one's willingness to improve.

That, as I say, is Delbert Earle's stated opinion. As in many things he says, it is shot through with discrepancy. I have it on good authority that Delbert Earle once tried leaving *his* underwear on the floor. His wife, in her superior wisdom, recognized the gesture for what it was and simply ignored it. The pile grew and grew. After a week or so, Delbert Earle had no clean underwear. One evening when his wife wasn't around, he picked up the pile and took it to the washing machine. She never said a word to Delbert Earle and he never got credit for that particular bad habit. Still, he thinks the principle is sound.

Personally, I'm of the opinion that Delbert Earle's problem is one of faulty execution. So I am looking for minor bad habits that don't incur the wrath (or smug superiority) of my dear wife. I don't smoke big, smelly cigars, but occasionally I go out into the back yard beyond my wife's hearing and utter a mild expletive. That will do for a start. I am also considering sauerkraut on my hot dogs. I hate sauerkraut on my hot dogs, so that would be a good bad habit to have, and one I could easily give up when the need arises.

Any suggestions? Delbert Earle and I would welcome them. As you probably surmise from the above, we both need help.

Delbert Earle Has His Fingers Crossed

When graduation time rolls around each year, our thoughts turn to the life of the mind, the rigorous pursuit of knowledge, the quest for truth and beauty. At my friend Delbert Earle's house, there is more than passing interest in intellectual commerce. It is accompanied by prayer and supplication.

Thousands of young people graduate each year from one level of schooling or another. They even have graduation exercises in elementary school, and if I remember sixth grade correctly, I know why. In my school, the teachers were glad to get rid of us and send us on to that half-school, half-hormone-management rite of passage called junior high. In one elementary I heard about, they give out honorary degrees at graduation. They should probably go to the sixth grade teachers, who could opt for either the degree or combat pay.

Whatever level they are commencing from, the most important thing for all these graduates is that they finally made it. Some will have made it with flying colors. Others will have gotten through by the skin of their teeth. In the case of Delbert Earle's boy, Elrod, it appears to be a skin-of-the-teeth thing. It's going right down to the wire, and the obstacle standing between Elrod and his diploma is "The Rime of the Ancient Mariner."

Elrod and the English language enjoy only a passing acquaintance, at least as far as grammar and punctuation are concerned. And Elrod seems convinced that Literature is simply a category on "Jeopardy," to be avoided at all costs by the contestants. Elrod does fine with such things as his stereo. He knows exactly where the volume knob is and how to turn it up. He can handle things like the stereo because he doesn't have to read the directions.

Elrod's English teacher, faced with the prospect of having the pleasure of his company in class for another year, has worked with him diligently. He hovers on the verge of passing the course, and he needs just a bit of extra credit to push him over the brink. Thus, "The Rime of the Ancient Mariner." His teacher doesn't insist that he understand it, only that he recite it. And unquestionably, Elrod doesn't understand it. His description of Samuel Taylor Coleridge, author of the

"Rime," is "a truly weird dude."

Elrod paces the floor of his room reciting: "Water, water everywhere and how the boards do shrink." Then he calls down the hall: "Daddy, if there's so much water, why do the boards shrink? I thought boards shrink when they dry out."

Delbert Earle calls back: "Don't worry about it, Elrod. Just stick to the script."

Delbert Earle and his wife are trying to have positive thoughts about the situation — good kharma, as Elrod puts it. Delbert Earle's wife has gone out and purchased a new dress for graduation. Delbert Earle has bought a new tie for himself. Elrod announced at supper that as a graduation present, he wants new mag wheels for his Trans-Am. But Delbert Earle is holding off on that purchase for the time being, just in case.

Delbert Earle maintains an outward air of stern expectation in the face of Elrod's challenge, but he harbors secret sympathies, too. He was, at best, a middling student in his days of high school matriculation. He passed senior English by the skin of his teeth, and he has suspected through the years that it was as much an act of mercy on the part of his teacher, Miz Pirtley, as it was any academic achievement on his. When she considered the prospect of having him in class for another year, she probably decided she had enjoyed about all of that she could stand for one lifetime. He has been eternally grateful.

Over the years, Delbert Earle has pretty much turned out all right. He married a smart girl, got a good job, and has been a good husband and father and a responsible citizen. He's acted the fool a few times, as we all have. But a few times, tempted to act like a Damfool, he has taken the path of responsibility, partly because he remembered that folks like Miz Pirtley had mercy on him back yonder in high school. Not long ago, he went by Miz Pirtley's house (she is retired now) and thanked her.

Delbert Earle hasn't told Elrod about Miz Pirtley. He's saving that for after graduation. For now, he's holding his breath and crossing his fingers and reciting lines from "The Rime of the Ancient Mariner" in his sleep. He recalls that the poem mentions an albatross, and Delbert Earle thinks he knows why Coleridge wrote that. He probably had a teenage son in peril at graduation time.

Elephants at the Kitchen Window

M y friend Delbert Earle, while certainly not part of what he calls the "egghead intelligentsia," occasionally comes up with some some gem of wisdom so pristine that it bears repeating. This is one of those occasions.

Delbert Earle called me on the phone and said, "A perfect marriage has one of each."

"One of each what?" I wanted to know.

"One of each everything."

"Oh," I said. "You mean that opposites attract."

"Not only that," said Delbert Earle, "exact opposites attract the best."

"Ah," said I, "then you have the perfect

marriage."

"Indeed!"

Delbert Earle went on at some length to enumerate the polar opposites in his marriage. His wife is neat, he is sloppy. His wife likes rutabagas, he hates them. His wife reads poetry, he reads fishing catalogs. He is a great sleeper. His wife is not.

He was reading in the paper where some scientists have found that you grow while you're asleep. "If that's so," Delbert Earle's wife said to him, "you should be nine and a half feet tall." Now, Delbert Earle doesn't sleep all the time. He simply gets eight good hours a night, then he bounds out of bed rarin' to go. But when he sleeps, it is industrial strength snoozing. Rip Van Winkle could take lessons. His wife uses ear plugs.

Delbert Earle says that in any lasting marriage, there is one heavy sleeper and one light sleeper. If two of the same kind marry, one of them will change — especially if both start out as heavy sleepers — or the marriage will not survive. Every marriage requires one light sleeper. After all, somebody has to hear those things that go bump in the night, like elephants trying to get in the kitchen window.

Delbert Earle says heavy sleepers get to be that way because of something he calls the Immutable Theory of Energy. I think he got it out of Popular Mechanics and applied it to human biology. He believes that we are all born with a certain amount of energy, and we spend our lives using it up. He says we can't get any more than we originally had, but we can control how fast we use what we do have. And he says he's a heavy sleeper because he's conserving his energy.

Light sleepers, he opines, were all born with

more energy than heavy sleepers, so they don't have to be so careful about conserving. His wife is the light sleeper in the family, ever attuned to night noises — dripping faucets, creaking joists, their boy Elrod's car easing into the driveway an hour late, the heavy tread of elephants outside the kitchen window. That's all fine, says Delbert Earle. He trusts his wife to handle these things while he's conserving energy. And he has finally convinced her not to wake him when she hears elephants at the kitchen window. So far, none have gotten in, or at least that's what Delbert Earle thinks. After all, he's been asleep. He has found no elephant tracks in the sink or peanut hulls on the kitchen floor.

Naturally, I am fascinated when Delbert Earle shares these nuggets of wisdom with me, and I try to bring what I can to the discussion. My contribution when he phoned was to share what professor Barry Hannah told me when I was taking writing courses in college. Barry had only one rule for writing stories. He called it the "Barry Hannah One Wacko Rule."

Barry said you could have only one wacko character in a story. The other characters had to be sane and straight and logical — a dose of reality against which you could judge the wacko character's wackiness. If you had more than one wacko, you couldn't tell what was lunacy and what wasn't. If you don't believe that, get two of your wackiest friends together sometime and just sit back and listen. Their conversation will be highly entertaining, but bizarre: in the words of the Kris Kristofferson song, "a walking contradiction, partly truth and partly fiction." Where the two diverge, it's impossible to tell.

A marriage, I averred to my friend Delbert

Earle, is just like a story. It can only stand one wacko. Get two of the same kind in a marriage, and it's headed for trouble, because neither partner can keep the other straight. If one has book learning, the other must possess common sense. If one is an optimist, the other must be a pessimist. If one sleeps the sleep of the dead, the other must be attuned to the presence of elephants at the kitchen window.

"How true, how true," Delbert Earle said. Then he thought for a moment and added, "but Professor Hannah's theory doesn't apply to my marriage. It doesn't have a wacko."

"Oh?" I replied, and hung up.

Delbert Earle and the World of Work

Y ou don't work, you're a writer," says my friend Delbert Earle. His idea of work is anything in which you lift, tote, fetch, hammer, dig, explode, or stand around a hole in the ground watching somebody else do one of the above.

"But writing is hard work," I protest. "I sometimes sweat profusely when I'm writing. I lose sleep. I have occasionally broken down in tears. Have you ever had to use a jackhammer on writer's block?"

"Okay," says Delbert Earle, "maybe writing falls into the general category of work, but it does not fit my definition of honest labor. Have you ever shed blood in the course of your writing work?"

"Well," says I, "I do sometimes cut myself on the edge of a sheet of paper. It is a very painful sort of wound, Delbert Earle."

"Sonny Boy," says Delbert Earle with a chortle (I really hate it when he chortles), "that doesn't count. Nothing less than something that requires stitches really qualfies as a job-related injury. Have you ever filed for workmen's compensation?"

"No," I admitted. "I never have."

"Well, then."

This is one subject on which I and Delbert Earle, who is my very good friend and a person I admire and respect greatly, have never been able to agree. Ever since I quit my day job to stay home and write, he has been skeptical. Since then, he has taken to calling me "Sonny Boy." We are about the same age, so it's not like an older fellow calling a younger fellow "Sonny Boy." No, I think it has something to do with his regard for my vocation.

So it was with some trepidation that I rushed over to Delbert Earle's house to tell him that I have finished a large writing project on which I invested more than three years of sweat, tears, and occasional paper cuts. Give Delbert Earle credit, he was gracious. Congratulatory. He looks forward to reading what I have written. But then he said, "Three years? You must have had a lot of writer's block." There is no use in trying to explain.

Maybe I bear some responsibility for Delbert Earle's skewed opinion of what it takes to write. He once asked me, "Sonny Boy, how do you write a book?"

I replied, "You stare out the window until you think up something, and then you write it down. Then you stare out the window some more, think up something else, and write that down. You keep doing that over and over until you've thought up everything you're going to think up, then you write THE END and send it off to your publisher." Did I create a false impression here?

Well, as I say, Delbert Earle was gracious and congratulatory. And he had some news of his own. He got a promotion where he works. I, too, was gracious and congratulatory.

It seems that his boss called him in and told him to show up the next morning in dress shirt and tie, because they were going to make him a coordinator. He rushed home and took his wife and boy Elrod out to dinner and bought Elrod a pair of Air Jordans.

The next morning, he showed up properly attired. He spent a couple of hours in Human Resources, where they signed him up for a 401K and a Stress Management Course. Then after lunch, he started his new office job. There are two kinds of people in this office, expediters and co-ordinators. An expediter, he learned, is someone who takes confusion and turns it into chaos. And a coordinator sits between two expediters. All af-ternoon, these expediters sent folks galloping off in all directions, and Delbert Earle spent all his time trying to get them straightened out. At the end of the day, Delbert Earle went in to see his boss. "Bossman," he said, "we need to get rid of these expediters."

"Well," said the boss, "we paid a manage-ment consultant thousands of dollars to study the place, and he said we need expediters. So we'll have to keep 'em until we get our money's worth."

So Delbert Earle said, "Bossman, if it's okay with you, I'd just as soon go back to what I was doing before."

The boss said, "All right, but if you'd stick around a few more days, you could have my job. I'm retiring on disability." And it was then that Delbert Earle noticed this bad tic his boss has.

So Delbert Earle went back to doing what he did before.

When he recounted the story to me, I said, "Aha! So you took a job in which you didn't lift, tote, fetch, hammer, dig, explode, or stand around a hole in the ground. You weren't doing honest labor!"

"Yeah, Sonny Boy," said Delbert Earle, "but it didn't take me three years to figure it out."

A Case of the Sartorially Challenged

My friend the deputy was telling me that lots of folks who come to court these days just don't seem to care. I've done a little first-hand research, and I'm inclined to agree with him.

My deputy friend has been in the law enforcement business for a good many years. He is a dedicated lawman and a keen observer of humankind. His observations on the physical appearance of court attendees — based on his frequent duty as a bailiff — are thoughtfully considered and more than a little tinged with sadness over the current state of sartorial affairs.

My friend the deputy says that when he first started out in law enforcement, people who went to court for any reason tried to look their best. They might not have much, but they wore the best thing they could pull out of the closet or borrow from a friend or relative. Coat and tie for the men, dress for the women. There seemed to be an unwritten dress code, dictated by the notion that if you were accused of running afoul of the law, you ought not to *look* like you had. When the judge and jury gazed upon your countenance, you wanted to give the appearance of a fine, respectable, upstanding citizen who was possessed of a hair brush, a workable razor, and at least one set of Sunday-go-to-meeting clothes. If your fate hung in the balance, the least little thing might tip the scales, including your packaging.

Alas, says my deputy friend, that no longer seems to be the case. Lots of folks show up in court — especially criminal court — looking like something the dog dragged in. Women appear in halter tops and one-size-too-small blue jeans, men in scruffy pants and open-necked shirts that appear to have gone through the wash at the factory, but not since. Hair (including facial) and fingernails show signs of long neglect and the general state of cleanliness seems to cry for a good scrubbing in a backyard washtub.

What is the effect of all this slovenliness? The defendant has entered a bold black mark against his or her name before the first word is uttered. The judge — freshly scrubbed and spiffily attired in black robe and judicial demeanor, looks down upon a poor pleader at the bar of justice whose appearance seems to say, "Aw, go ahead and send me to jail. At least they have uniforms and showers." And jurors, who generally arrive in court looking presentable, get the general impression of someone who doesn't give much of a hoot and might not be trusted to tell the truth if asked.

I decided, based on my deputy friend's assessment, to see for myself. I looked in on a session of criminal Superior Court in a county in our area. It was the first day of session and the purpose was to set the calendar of cases to be heard during the coming week. So everybody who had been accused of a felony or serious misdemeanor was there — or, at least, supposed to be there. Some of the defendants didn't bother to show up, forgot, overslept, or had fled the county. The judge sent deputies looking for them.

Of those who did appear, there were a few who looked as if they had made a good-faith effort to put on a good appearance. These weren't necessarily members of the Chamber of Commerce Board of Directors, just ordinary citizens who realized that first impressions are important. The rest were ill-clad, unkempt and generally skuzzy-looking. They might have been nice folks, the kind you would invite to Sunday dinner with the preacher, but they didn't look the part. They were, I'm afraid, not giving themselves their best chance of acquittal.

My friend Delbert Earle agrees with me that the way you look can have a great deal to do with the way you feel about yourself and about how others regard you. He remembers going into the Army right out of high school — a cool dude with a slouch and a swagger, shirt unbuttoned about halfway down his torso, peg-legged jeans, a ducktailed haircut, and a comb sticking out of a back pocket.

The Army cut off his hair, confiscated his comb, shipped his civilian clothes home, and gave him a uniform that he was required to keep buttoned at all times. They taught him how to make up a bunk with square corners, correct his posture, and eat everything on his tray in the mess hall. He no longer looked like a poor imitation of Elvis Presley, and the times he acted like it, he was made to regret it. The lessons stayed with him long after he left the service.

Delbert Earle's wife, who picked up where the Army left off, says there are a number of things about him she set out to change, but couldn't. But he does usually look presentable and still cleans his plate and is able to make a bed with square corners. He has never been summoned to criminal court. But if he were, he would pass sartorial muster. "Yeah," she says, "he'd be all right as long as he didn't open his mouth." Oh well. Clothes, I suppose, don't entirely make the man.

Delbert Earle's Spring Fix-up

When spring clean-up, fix-up, paint-up time rolls around, my friend Delbert Earle always feels self-congratulatory. Invariably, he hasn't cleaned, fixed or painted anything — though his wife has a considerable list of projects tacked to the door of his workshop — but he has spent all winter getting ready. And as always, he may spring into action at any moment.

Delbert Earle believes that any job around the house can be accomplished with a handful of basic tools — hammer, screwdriver, monkey wrench, pliers, first-aid kit — and three products. At the risk of sounding commercial, I will name them: Liquid Nails, WD-40, and Campbell's Soup cans. I'm sure there are other equally efficacious products that would substitute agreeably, but Delbert Earle is adamant about those particular ones. He has learned from experience.

Delbert Earle first tried Liquid Nails when Joe down at Joe's Hardware recommended it. "It's just what it says, Delbert Earle," said Joe, "you slap a little bit of that stuff between two things you want to hold together, and by golly, it stays."

Delbert Earle first used Liquid Nails to mend a wooden patio chair. Over the ensuing years, the chair rotted. One day, Delbert Earle's dog Old Shep leaped into the chair and it collapsed. Every joint failed except the one where the Liquid Nails had been used. It was still holding firm, impervious to wind and weather.

Another time, squirrels started eating on a bird feeder in the back yard. Delbert Earle applied Liquid Nails to the damaged area. The squirrels developed dental problems and moved on.

Delbert Earle has even used Liquid Nails for automotive repair. Or at least, his wife has. A strip of chrome was coming off the edge of a door on Delbert Earle's old pickup truck. He kept threatening to take it to an auto body repair shop, but procrastination is one of Delbert Earle's most endearing qualities. Finally, while he was off at work one day, his wife went out with the Liquid Nails and glued the sucker back on. It's still there. I don't believe the "jaws of life" could get it off.

It was also Delbert Earle's wife who discovered the many uses of WD-40. Great-grandaddy Birtwhistle left them an antique wind-up wall clock when he passed on, and Delbert Earle's wife hung it in the entrance hall. She would wind it and start the pendulum swinging, and within about ten minutes, it would stop. When she asked a cousin about the clock, he said, "Aw, that old thing never did run."

She first tried getting Delbert Earle to fix the clock. He would start the pendulum swinging, and when it would quit ten minutes later, he would say, "Hon', it ain't supposed to do that." Then she took it to a clock repair expert. "Oh," he said, "I can fix anything that ticks." He kept the clock for two months and finally returned it in frustrated defeat. So in desperation, Delbert Earle's wife sprayed the works with WD-40. The clock repair expert was appalled and predicted that the clock would fall apart. But that was ten years ago and the clock has run like a charm ever since.

And then there are tin cans. Any can of similar size would work just fine, but Delbert Earle insists that Campbell Soup cans are special. He uses them for things like holding nails. He has a can marked LITTLE BITTY NAILS, one marked ABOUT AVERAGE NAILS, and a third labeled GREAT OLD BIG NAILS. He has a can designated for machine screws, another for wood screws, another for washers, and still another for band-aids. He uses a lot of band-aids in his workshop.

Clean-up fix-up paint-up time at Delbert Earle's house occasionally gets delayed because another project gets in the way. A couple of years ago, Delbert Earle got distracted by letter-writing. He wrote to NASA, suggesting they take Liquid Nails,

WD-40, and lots of Campbell Soup cans along on the space shuttle. He said that with those items and a pair of tin snips, you could repair anything. Delbert Earle waited patiently for a reply acknowledging his brilliance, but NASA never responded. However, within months of his letter, a shuttle went up and astronauts fixed the Hubble telescope. Delbert Earle is convinced there is a connection. He expects to read any day in the paper that NASA is having tin cans made on special order for several hundred dollars apiece.

As another spring approaches, Delbert Earle is again feeling self-congratulatory. He has his supplies in hand and a lengthy list of uses for them. As his friend, I look forward to hearing reports of his sterling accomplishments. Then again, I'm glad Delbert Earle's wife knows how to use all that stuff.

Elrod's Laws of Physics, Simplified

My friend Delbert Earle is in something of a state of shock these days. His boy, Elrod, who finished high school by the skin of his teeth, has gone on to college and seems to be handling the rigors of higher education fairly well. But what really surprises Delbert Earle is that Elrod passed physics last semester.

Delbert Earle is surprised because Elrod never showed the slightest interest in or aptitude for any kind of science in high school. He gave cursory notice to biology, but only because there was stuff in it about girls. The other sciences were as foreign as Latin or Swahili. The closest he ever got to the laws of physics was figuring out the proper English on a two-rail bank shot down at the billiard hall. So when Elrod arrived back home for the summer and announced that he had passed physics, Delbert Earle went into a swoon.

I agree with Delbert Earle that Elrod's achievement is splendid news. But I was not so surprised as he. I reminded Delbert Earle that Elrod had, unwittingly perhaps, been exposed to the laws of physics in a dramatic way some few years ago. I speak of the Harmonic Convergence Affair.

It happened one Saturday night about 7:30 when Elrod was upstairs getting ready for a date. Delbert Earle knew that was what he was doing because there was no hot water and the air reeked of Aqua Velva. Elrod had his stereo turned up full blast and was listening to his favorite romantic CD, by a band that sounds like it is fighting the War of 1812 and losing badly. At one point in the recording, one member of the band does something with a guitar that sounds akin to a cat in heat on the back fence at midnight.

At that very moment, Delbert Earle's wife stepped out the back door onto the tail of Old Shep the Wonder Dog. Old Shep let out a howl, the guitar let out a howl, and things began to come apart all over the house. A big crack appeared in the fireplace, the refrigerator door flew open, and Delbert Earle's painting of Niagara Falls fell off the bedroom wall.

Delbert Earle called the fire department, which in turn called in a professor from the University. "Harmonic convergence," he pronounced.

And Delbert Earle said, "Lordy, we need Elrod and Old Shep in Bosnia, looking for mines."

So, Elrod has had some experience with physics, and obviously, it rubbed off on him. Elrod not only passed his college course, he seems to have taken a genuine interest in the subject.

Delbert Earle is trying to encourage this. "What do you do with this physics stuff?" he asks.

"You figure out things," Elrod answers.

To illustrate, Elrod shares with Delbert Earle a physics thing he got off the Internet, submitted by a brilliant student from some big eastern university: *"When a cat is dropped, it always lands on its feet, and when toast is dropped, it always lands with the buttered side facing down. I propose to strap buttered toast to the back of a cat; the two will hover, spinning inches above the ground. With a giant buttered cat array, a high-speed monorail could easily link New York with Chicago."*

"Eureka!" says Delbert Earle. It's a word he heard a mad scientist character utter in an old film on American Movie Classics. Armed with such knowledge, Delbert Earle thinks, Elrod may achieve scientific greatness.

"But there's more," Elrod says, handing his father this gem from another fellow student: *"If an infinite number of rednecks riding in an infinite number of pickup trucks fire an infinite number of shotgun rounds at an infinite number of highways signs, they will eventually produce all of the world's great literary works in Braille."*

"Double eureka!" Delbert Earle cries joyfully.

And then there's this one, which explains why yawning is contagious: *"You yawn to equalize pressure on your eardrums. This pressure change outside your eardrums unbalances other people's ear pressures, so they must yawn to even it out."*

Well, the long and short of it is that Delbert Earle is enraptured by Elrod's new-found scientific wisdom. He is considering a second job to put money aside for graduate school. Massachusetts Institute of Technology, perhaps. Or CalTech. He has a vision: Elrod as president of Intel or Microsoft, sending his parents on vacations to the Mediterranean.

His wife gently reminds Delbert Earle that Elrod can't change a flat tire and doesn't know a screwdriver from a socket wrench. But that will come, Delbert Earle insists. And when Elrod is president of Intel or Microsoft, he won't need to.

He Stares Out the Window a Lot

Summoning the Courage to Write

Writer friend Ralph Keyes tells a story about his son's first day in the first grade. The teacher asked the students what kind of work their fathers do. When he got to Ralph's son, he said, "He stares out the window a lot." It says a lot about the writing life.

Ralph has written a thoughtful and incisive book, *The Courage to Write*, in which he analyzes the hang-ups writers have about putting words on the page and offers some helpful, inspirational advice on how to overcome them. He and I agree that one measure of a writer's courage is the willingness to stare out the window a lot. Too often, writers are so impatient to get the words down on paper or computer screen, we don't put enough effort into making sure the words are well-chosen. Staring out the window time is when the real writing gets done. Everything else is just typing.

It's especially true for writers of fiction. We fill imaginary worlds with invented people, then set them loose to rattle around inside that imaginary world until they make a story. When we stare out the window, we see through the actual world outside and into the imaginary world we've created. Then we enter that world of our characters and follow them at a respectful distance, writing down what they say, do and think.

As a fairly visible writer, I get a good number of inquiries from prospective writers, seeking advice on both the art and craft of writing. I'm a little wary of telling other folks how to do things, but here are a few lessons I've learned that may be valuable to others:

Take time to stare out the window, figuratively as well as literally. Writing can happen at any time if you are truly engaged with your characters. When you are occupied with some otherwise unrelated activity, the imaginary stew you are cooking is bubbling quietly in a secret recess in your mind. When I was writing my first novel, I learned that if I got hung up on something, the best thing to do was go jogging. Invariably, at mid-run, a solution would appear out of nowhere. My neighbors got used to me suddenly yelling, "Eureka!" as I passed.

Be diligent. Write at least a little every day. Especially for a fiction writer, it's important to visit the world of your story on a daily basis. If you do that, your characters take on a life of their own. A successful novelist I know says she sets aside an hour a day to write. Sometimes it stretches to two hours, but on most days, an hour is all she can spare from the other demands on her life. You'll be surprised at how quickly the pages pile up if you write for an hour a day.

Write the whole story. There are lots of folks who are capable of writing a book, but few who will. What separates the doers from the wannabes is patient persistence. A publisher may love the first couple of chapters and outline, but the real question is, "Can this writer stay the course?" For first-time novelists especially, it's important to be able to show the publisher a full, well-rounded story.

Be careful how you seek and accept

advice. Writing seriously, especially the first time out, is a scary business. We want someone to say, "Yeah. It's okay. You're doing it right." Some writers find that a mentor or a writing group can provide insight and encouragement. But writing is essentially a lonely affair. Ultimately, you have to listen to your own heart and follow your instincts. Novelist Barry Hannah says that when we write fiction, we peel away layer after layer of flesh until we get down to the place where it bleeds, and that's where we find truth. That's the painful path to honest writing, and it's hard to do with someone looking over your shoulder. After the manuscript is done, a literary agent who may represent you or an editor who may buy your book are qualified to give you an evaluation. Until then, be cautious.

When you have finished the writing, then take time to research the publishing process. This is the point where art meets commerce. Your local library or bookstore has good resource books that will tell you how to get an agent and how to approach publishers. Writers conferences and seminars can also be good places to meet agents and editors and network with fellow writers. Again, be patiently persistent. Publishable manuscripts get published, but often not by the first editor who reads them.

Writing is both art and craft. The art comes from the heart and the craft comes from the head. Both the art and the craft depend on applying the seat of the pants to the seat of the chair. And taking time to stare out the window.

Coming Home to the Paper

When the late Bear Bryant left Texas A&M to become football coach at his alma mater, Alabama, in 1957, he said, "Mama called and I came home." That's sort of the way I felt in 1996 when I became a regular contributor to *The Charlotte Observer.*

What became a forty-year career in journalism began with newspapering at my hometown Alabama weekly, *The Elba Clipper,* in 1956. I had long been fascinated by what went on in the ink-stained bowels of the paper — where people took events and ideas and turned them into words that everybody could read and share.

When I was eight years old, I appeared at the back door of the *Clipper* office one day and asked the editor for a job. He told me to come back when I was a little older. Five years later, on my second try, he hired me. I went to work in the back shop as a "printer's devil" — an apprentice wretch to whom the printer, according to tradition, "gave the devil." It was in the days when the text of the newspaper was set on a clanking linotype machine that occasionally erupted like Vesuvius and showered the printer and shop with molten metal. Headlines and advertisements were set largely by hand. I learned the trade by hand — getting ink under my fingernails and in my blood, experiencing words as physical things that you could hold and admire, letter by letter.

I learned that newspapering is an altogether human enterprise, fraught with human frailty. I dumped the entire front page of one edition on the floor an hour before press time and had to put it back together line by line from the jumbled pile of type. The press ran late that day, but I knew every sacred word of the front page before it was printed.

Later, I added some minor writing duties — high school news and sports and the like — and learned first-hand the agony of the typographical error. One good citizen named Mr. Dunaway had been to Tuscaloosa to watch an Elba boy play football for Bear Bryant. I wrote, "When Dyess scored, Mr. Dunaway stood up and *rotted* for the former Elba star." It got printed that way. I learned to check my work, word for word.

The editor, godlike creature that he was, was not immune. Elba's principal industry was and is a truck trailer factory. In a special edition honoring the company and its founding family, the editor referred to the family matriarch as the "*vile* (as opposed to vice) president of Dorsey Trailers."

Most of all, I learned about the power of words — to inform, to entertain, to educate, and occasionally to disturb. That's one of the primary functions of newspapers — to disturb. To shake the community by the scruff of the neck and make people think.

I intended, there in my adolescence, to be a newspaperman. But alas, a fellow built a radio station in Elba and I was lured away from the *Clipper* by the siren song of broadcasting. I became a disc jockey. My friends and family could actually hear *me* on the radio. And I could dedicate songs to sweethearts, including mine. I worked my way through college disc jockeying and then became a television journalist, first in Montgomery and then in Charlotte.

But I never forgot the newspaper. So when I wrote my first novel, *Home Fires Burning*, my hero was a cantankerous old newspaperman named

Jake Tibbetts who enjoyed nothing so much as disturbing his small southern hometown. And I tried to capture Jake's reverence for words and his sense of what a newspaper means to a community.

Jake comes to newspapering reluctantly and ill-prepared. Writing confounds him until he discovers its essential secret: "Most of the business involved having something worth saying, and the rest depended on saying it simply." He tacks a message to himself on the wall above his typewriter: "CHEW ADJECTIVES THOROUGHLY AND ESCHEW ADVERBS ALTOGETHER." And then he commences to "get the town's bowels in an uproar." In his sixty-fifth year he muses that he "had always spoken his mind, even when it hurt, even when he had been dead wrong. That was what a newspaper was supposed to do."

I suppose I thought of Jake, as I created him and then watched and listened while he told his story, as the newspaperman I might have been. But I wasn't. Roads led elsewhere until I reached the point in mid-life when I left daily television journalism to be a full-time writer. Writing, I decided, was what I want to do when I grow up.

So, I went back to the paper, where it all began. It didn't make me a newspaperman. That honored title goes to reporters and editors and all of the other folks who do the daily work of taking events and ideas and turning them into words we can all read and share. But in the four years since I began the weekly contribution, I've been mighty glad to be in their company. Mama called and I came home.

Movies: The Hard Work of Making Magic

The late film great Spencer Tracy had three rules for becoming a successful actor: show up on time; remember your lines; don't bump into the furniture.

I think Mr. Tracy was being too modest. As one of the giants of the movie industry, he knew full well that it takes a great deal more than that to transform the words of a script into memorable performance. I got to thinking about it after seeing the *The Green Mile*, which stars my favorite actor, Tom Hanks. I remembered how he started off years ago playing silly comedy roles with great fun and flair, and how he has transformed himself into a dramatic actor of enormous range. He is, arguably, the best in his business today. I'm sure he shows up on time, remembers his lines, and doesn't bump into the furniture. But that's just the beginning.

You can always tell a bad actor on TV or in the movies, because you never get past the notion that he's an actor playing a part. A good actor is so adept at what he's doing that we're willing to suspend belief and let him lead us into the unreal world he's creating. And that's especially difficult for a really well-known actor to do. Tom Hanks is huge. A superstar. Won't he always be Tom Hanks up there on the screen? Well, no. When he works his magic, we believe that he's a guard on death row at a 1935 Louisiana prison, or an Army captain on the beach at Normandy, or a Philadelphia lawyer dying of AIDS, or that wonderful combination of idiot and savant, Forrest

Gump.

Compounding the actor's difficult task is the controlled chaos that is a movie set. It involves a small army of talented people who never appear in front of the camera — cinematographers, makeup artists, lighting and sound technicians, directors, prop managers, and the like. They're all there, looking on intently, as the actors play out a scene while the camera rolls. The actors have to block all that out, to exist only in the tiny world that the lens creates, the one we will see when we view the finished product. It is an artificial world, but the actor must convince us that it is the only thing that is real.

And that's not the only challenge. Movies are never filmed in the sequence in which they're seen by the audience. If a script calls for several scenes in a graveyard, interspersed through the length of the film, the company will film all of them before moving on to the next location because of the time and expense of transporting equipment and people from one place to another. Thus, the actor may be filming a scene this morning for the middle of the movie, and another this afternoon for the beginning. A good actor knows exactly where each scene fits and how his character is changing as the story progresses. So no matter how out-of-sequence the work is, he's true to the role at each moment.

It's not even necessary, in the strictest sense of the word, for the actor to follow Spencer Tracy's advice about remembering lines. One producer I know says that actors take three approaches to learning the part. One is to scrupulously memorize each night the lines that will be delivered the next day and arrive at the set totally prepared. Another is to memorize nothing the night before, but learn the lines on the set just before delivering them, so as to be more spontaneous. And some actors do neither. I observed this on a movie set awhile back when one of the key actors kept flubbing his lines — exasperating the director, crew, and other cast members who had to keep shooting scenes over and over. But when the movie appeared in finished form, this particular actor was terrific. When he finally got it down, he filled up the role in a powerful, believable way.

A really good actor has a sense of the whole movie and helps make everything and everyone around him better. I watched James Woods at work on a movie several years ago and marveled at the knowledge of his craft that he brought to the set. Woods not only knew his part, he knew everybody else's — how the action was moving about him, where people were supposed to be and when. He was like a second director, helping things run smoothly, putting less experienced cast members at ease and helping them do things they might not have thought they were capable of doing. I would bet good money that Tom Hanks does the same on any set where he's working.

Much of the movie business is about deal-making — matching up this hot script with that hot star and director, convincing a network or studio to plunk down wheelbarrows full of money to bring off a production. But at some point the deal-making ends and the movie-making begins. When good people do good work, it creates a magical experience that is like no other. And for my money, Tom Hanks does it better than just about anybody.

The Simplest of Joys: A Book for Christmas

If you watch the "Hallmark Hall of Fame" movies on television, you know that the commercials for Hallmark Cards are equally as entertaining as the films themselves. They're exquisite little mini-dramas that tug at your heartstrings and make you want to rush to the store for cards that say just the right thing to a special person.

One of my favorites is about a working mom and two small boys. Mom drags in from the office at the end of a grueling day to be met in the front hallway by her sons, holding a favorite book, begging her to read to them. But Mom has lots to do — dishes, laundry, etc. And Dad is busy on the phone, taking care of business he brought home. Finally, at the end of the evening, Mom puts down her basket of laundry and curls up in bed with the boys to read from a childhood classic about a little railroad engine. *Chug-chug, toot-toot.* As she turns one page, she finds a card (a Hallmark, of course) from the two boys and Dad that tells her what a great gal she is and how much they appreciate all she does for them. If you can watch that without feeling a little misty-eyed, you're a tougher bird than I.

When I see that commercial, it makes me nostalgic for the days of our daughters' childhood when Paulette and I read to them from *The Three Little Kittens* and *The Little Ballerina* and the like. Those were special moments, propped up in bed, or snuggled in an easy chair in the den — as special for parent as for youngster, sharing warmth as well as an imaginative experience. They are moments I wish for every parent and child. And there's no better time to start than at Christmas.

As a youngster, I always got books for Christmas — from Santa, from relatives. Books were essential and natural in my large, extended family. My grandmother's attic was full of the Tom Swift and Bobbsey Twins and Tarzan books my mother and three uncles had devoured as children. My siblings and cousins and I were read to as children, and we're all avid readers today. We all looked forward to Christmas and a new supply of books we could devour and pass around.

Why is reading to a child so important? First of all, it's just plain fun. A good tale well told is a joy to the spirit. And childhood should have its share of pure, unadulterated fun.

Secondly, reading is the single most important stimulus to the imagination. Imagination, I tell children, is what you see when your eyes are closed. When you read a book, or are read to, the words on the page create a rich, vibrant world inside your mind — intriguing people, fascinating places, incredible adventures. That helps form the habit of imagining — of picturing in your mind how things *might be.* I believe most of the failures in this world are failures of imagination. It's not so much that we don't do what needs to be done, it's that we fail to imagine *how* it might be done. We Americans pride ourselves on our ingenuity and initiative. Those are both products of imagination. And if we're to continue as a nation that knows how to get things done, we need future generations of imaginers.

Thirdly, a book can be a great companion. We need never feel alone when we can enter the world of a book and engage ourselves with its people, places, events and ideas. As Benjamin Franklin once said, the most pitiable human condition is "a lonesome man on a rainy day who does not know how to read."

Thirdly, reading produces storytellers. And storytelling is how we pass along the myths and legends and histories and values of one generation to the next. I'm the only one of my extended family who has written a book, but all of the others had a hand in it. I grew up in a rich storytelling tradition in which my grandmother and parents and aunts and uncles told tales about each other and their forebears — some, I suspect, embellished for the sheer joy of the telling. I had a keen sense of the drama and comedy of their everyday lives, and that is why I could go on to create characters and stories of my own. I wouldn't be a writer without them.

Books, of course, can be of immense practical value. British novelist G.K. Chesterton was once asked what books he would like to have with him if he were stranded on a desert island. "Thomas's *Guide to Practical Shipbuilding*," he replied.

There is a vast canon of literature available to today's children, from the classics of the past to the wonderful contributions being made by today's authors. Give a child a book for Christmas, then sit down and read it to him or her. And make sure he or she has a library card. Long after the toys are broken and the clothes outgrown, those books — those simple joys — will keep on giving.

Some Idle Thoughts About Thoughts

I've been thinking about thinking.

What got me started was a quote I read from the late rocket scientist Wernher von Braun. He once said, "Basic research is when I'm doing what I don't know I'm doing."

Another word for what Dr. von Braun was talking about is "serendipity," which the dictionary defines as "the faculty of making fortunate and unexpected discoveries by accident." My dictionary goes on to say that the word was invented by 18th Century English man of letters Horace Walpole to describe the discoveries made by characters in his fairy tale, *The Three Princes of Serendip.* Walpole gave us a wonderful word that describes that magnificent feeling we get when something makes us say, "Eureka!"

Occasionally, I have a serendipitous thought. Often it involves some piece of writing I am doing, usually fictional. I tell my friends that as a fiction writer, I get to lie for a living. That's only partly right. In telling a tale, I create an imaginary world full of invented people. But what happens, and to whom it happens, must be believable enough for a reader to take a leap of faith into the story. In other words, it has to be "true" in the larger sense of the word. So I invent these characters and set them loose in their made-up world to bump up against each other and make sparks and create a story. My job is to follow along behind and write down what they do and say. I have to be willing to let them surprise me, and quite often, they do. "Well, I'll be darned," I might

231

say as I discover that a character has revealed an unexpected truth or galloped off in a direction I hadn't counted on — something that makes the character real and genuine. Serendipity. Or, as Dr. von Braun put it, basic research.

In order for serendipity to happen, I have to be quiet and still and patient. I have to visit my invented family every day and then watch and listen carefully. Sometimes what they say to me is a mere whisper. If I'm galloping about myself, making too much noise and dust, I miss it.

Sometimes they sneak up on me at unexpected and even inconvenient moments. It is not uncommon for my dear wife to see me wandering naked down the hallway from shower to office to jot down something before it escapes me. I have occasionally been jerked wide awake from deep sleep by an idea that has a perishable shelf-life and needs to be recorded immediately. Some years ago, I got a phone call in the middle of the night from one of the characters in the book I was writing at the time, passing along some vital information. At times I wonder if I, too, am not leading a fictional life.

Anyone who creates — and that's all of us — has experienced serendipity. It happens to scientists like Dr. von Braun when they give themselves time to putter about the laboratory asking that essential question, "What if?"

One of my favorite scientists is a fellow named Jack Kilby, who's credited (along with others) with inventing the microchip. It happened not long after he went to work for Texas Instruments back in the Fifties. The company was so small in those days that it shut down every summer for a couple of weeks for everybody to take vacation. But Jack hadn't been there long enough to earn any vacation, so while everybody else took off, he stayed and puttered in the lab. Nobody and nothing interrupted his thoughts. There was no office football pool, no gossip at the water cooler, no pressure of deadlines and quotas. Jack thought and thought, worked out things in his mind, tinkered and piddled. And by the time the other folks came back from vacation, he had worked out the basic concept of the microchip. It is arguably the biggest technological breakthrough of the last century, and it was born in the patient stillness of Jack Kilby's mind. Basic research. Serendipity.

There's a lesson there for all of us. We live boiler factory lives, dashing hither and yon, surrounding ourselves with noise and dust, and we don't take enough time to be quiet, to just think about things and hear whispers.

It's a common dilemma for many businesses. Folks are so busy meeting sales quotas and planning marketing schemes and going to meetings and writing memos and increasing widget production that there's no time for reasoned thought. I used to complain about it when I was in the news business. There seemed to be a deadline every few minutes, a breaking story every hour, gaping maws of space and time that had to be filled with words and pictures. We never had time to stop and think about why and how we did things. If we had, we might have done them differently.

I admit, I'm no paragon of virtue when it comes to thinking. I gallop about too much, often let my alligator mouth overload my hummingbird fanny, and set aside far too little of that patient quiet time. But occasionally, I am struck by an idea that comes out of nowhere and gives me great pleasure by its sheer novelty. Serendipity. Basic

research. And then I renew my vow to be a better, quieter thinker.

Thank you, Dr. von Braun

Storytelling with Uncle Walter

One thing I regret for today's young people
is that they never had the opportunity to
benefit from Walter Cronkite's delivery of
the television network evening news. He retired
from CBS in 1981, at age sixty-five. That's unfor-
tunate, because today, in his mid-eighties, he has
the energy and mental sharpness of a much
younger man. And television — make that journalism in general — could use his ideals, his intellectual curiosity, and his unique perspective.

I had the privilege of interviewing Walter
Cronkite before a large crowd in Charlotte not long
ago. It was an evening of wit and wisdom, none of
it mine. For an hour, I asked a few questions and
he dazzled me and the audience with his incredible grasp of what shapes our world and why.

The program was billed as "The Legacy of
the Twentieth Century." In my mind, it is the
"Cronkite Century." He lived through most of it
and saw it from a unique vantage point. He began his career as a newspaperman in Houston,
went on to cover World War Two and Moscow as a
United Press correspondent, and joined CBS in
1950. He has known the famous and infamous,
has been present at the great events.

He doesn't mind being called "Uncle Walter." During the thirty years he covered the news for CBS, he came to be known as America's television uncle. When he reported on the news of the day, you could count on knowing what was important and why. By doing his job accurately and fairly, he built up a reservoir of trust that any journalist would covet. What he told us on any given night might be bad news, but we left with the impression that bad things pass and that we would not only survive but endure.

Personally, I think one reason Walter Cronkite was so successful, so respected, so cherished by America is that he's a natural-born storyteller. After all, that's what the news is: stories. They're about people who are doing things, thinking things, that the rest of us need to know about. Uncle Walter had — still has — an eye and a nose for the human story behind any event. He was at his best when asking penetrating questions of the people who made news, and always doing it in a civil manner.

He's still a great storyteller and a genuinely funny man who doesn't mind humor at his own expense. He told the crowd about being on location, along with his wife Betsy, for the filming of a documentary. They were approached by a woman who said, "You look a lot like Walter Cronkite did before he died. Only he was thinner."

Cronkite said he had to turn away to keep from bursting out laughing. The woman turned to Betsy. "Walter Cronkite is dead, isn't he?" she asked.

"Oh yes," Betsy replied. "He died of thinness."

The first time I met Walter Cronkite was in the CBS newsroom in New York. My co-anchor at a Charlotte television station and I had been dispatched to film promotional announcements with Cronkite, whose network newscast followed ours. He was gracious and affable, willing to take time from a hectic news day to visit with the local guys. We got to talking about the TV news business and he picked up a copy of the *New York Times* from his desk. "The entire text of the CBS Evening News would only fill a third of the front page of the Times," he said.

Cronkite was and is an honest man. He recognized the limitations of the medium he worked in and wasn't bashful at all about saying so. His opinion, then and now, was that no one is a well-informed citizen if he or she depends solely on television for news. He gives television great credit for its immediacy, its emotional impact, its ability to put us on the scene of events large and small. Television is superb at giving us the "who, what, where, and when" of news — but it's not so good with the "how and why." For that, Uncle Walter says, you need print journalism: newspapers, books, magazines.

Television depends on pictures, and pictures are usually only part of the story, maybe even a minor part. There is a context to everything that happens, and often, the context is more important than what happened. Walter Cronkite tried mightily to provide context when he edited and anchored the CBS Evening News. He's honest enough to know and say that he was only partly successful.

Cronkite believes the essential role of journalism is to give us the tools we need to be responsible citizens. We can't act and decide responsibly unless we know. That involves news media that report honestly and fearlessly and citizens who care enough to inform themselves. We can all judge ourselves in that respect — journalists and citizens — by the standards Uncle Walter set.

Lost in Cyber-Limbo

One of my favorite features in my local newspaper, the *Charlotte Observer,* is "Q&A" — a daily smorgasbord of sometimes-useful but always interesting answers to questions that bedevil us. Want to know if Elvis is alive? Who's buried in Grant's tomb? Why moss grows on the north side of trees? Ask "Q&A" and you'll find out.

I, too have a question for "Q&A." What happens to things when computers eat them?

I've thought for the longest time that the answer was, "They go into cyberspace." But "Q&A" defined cyberspace not long ago as "the community formed by the interconnected computers of the world." That means when my computer eats something, it ends up in another, connected computer. Okay, I can live with that. But what if my computer isn't connected to another computer? The term "cyberspace" doesn't work here. Is there another place out there in the twilight zone, something like "cyber-limbo?" Please, "Q&A," put me at ease here.

I've been wondering about this from the first time I touched a computer. Several years ago, I worked in a newsroom that became computerized. A bunch of very smart people came in, took our clunky old typewriters away from us, and installed a computer system — one central electronic brain, fed by multiple terminals from which we news wretches could enter data. These very smart people taught us how the system was supposed to work and hired a computer guru to sit in an office upstairs and respond promptly if we had a problem.

Can you say, "crash?" It was a word we got used to right away. The system would, without warning or provocation, simply stop working. Sometimes our terminal screens would just go blank. At other times, the screens would fill with gibberish — the kinds of *@X##!!!* stuff you see in the comic strips to indicate cussing. In the middle of a busy day in a busy newsroom, this sort of thing can be, to say the least, disconcerting.

When a "crash" occurred, we would haul our old clunky typewriters out of the closet where we had hidden them and keep working while the guru and the very smart people huddled around the computer with their stethoscopes and incense-burners and coaxed it back to life. Then we would hide the typewriters again and resume our new life on the cutting edge of technology.

But "crashes," as awful as they were, weren't the worst. Occasionally, when the computer was humming away happily over in one corner, you would hear a howl of agony from some reporter over in another corner: "It's gone!" And indeed, whatever story the poor wretch had been working on had simply disappeared. We would immediately dial up the computer guru in his upstairs office (it quickly became clear why his office was upstairs, not in the newsroom) and say, "The computer did so-and-so." And the guru's inevitable response was, "It's not supposed to do that."

It was tough enough working with a computer that did things it wasn't supposed to do. But there was also the agony of lying awake at night, wondering what happened to all those news stories that simply went away.

I began to suspect the existence of some hidden dimension of time and space — something akin to a black hole or a quark — into which this material disappeared. I imagined a whirling void of sub-atomic bits and bytes, banging into each other, setting off millions of little cosmic explosions and creating all manner of physical and psychic mischief. Just think of the terrible stew it would make — all those news stories about wrecks, fires, stupid pet tricks and anti-social behavior, along with your nearly-finished spreadsheet, the term paper that was due tomorrow, and your letter to Aunt Martha. As Major Hoople used to say, "Gadzooks!" No wonder we have record heat and cold, eruptions of long-dead volcanoes, famine and pestilence, and general malaise among the populace.

Early in mankind's existence, we blamed aberrations in nature and human behavior on such things as black magic and unruly gods. Later on, we unleashed other forces. My grandmother spoke ominously of "the bomb." And now we have computers — more and more of them, running faster and faster, invading every nook and cranny of our lives. Are they stealing our words and numbers and sending them into something called "cyber-limbo?" If so, is cyber-limbo filling up? Are we on the verge of another "Big Bang?" Should we grab our ankles?

We won't know until we get an answer from "Q&A." Hurry, folks. We may be running out of time.

Writing One Agonizing Word at a Time

I t's true: 'tis easier to have written than it is to write.

My graduate school writing teacher, novelist Barry Hannah, laid that piece of wisdom on me twenty-five years ago, back when I *aspired* to be a writer. Now, I am one. But the truth still holds, now more than ever.

After three published novels, about which readers and critics have said mostly pleasant things, you'd think I would have this business down cold. But with each new effort, writing is the same wretched, painful process as the others have been. A character emerges full-blown in my imagination with what seems to be a compelling story. But the story goes on paper one agonizing word at a time. Writing is abominable work. The urge to write is a curse as much as a blessing.

So it's good for me to take a brief respite from writing once in awhile to remind myself of a couple of thoughts that should comfort any person who is doomed to write.

When I was handing in work in Barry Hannah's class at Alabama, he was kind enough to say that it showed some promise. "When you learn the big tricks," he said, "you'll do okay."

"What are the big tricks?" I asked.

"You have to learn those for yourself."

"How do you learn them?"

"By doing the work."

So I've done a good bit of the work since then, and I've learned a couple of big tricks. The biggest, I've decided, is learning to trust your reader. It sounds simple, but it's not.

I have to see a scene in my own mind before I can write about it — what the place looks like, who's there, how they move about, how they interact, what they say. The problem is trying to put what I see on paper so you'll see the same thing when you read the words. But the more I try to describe, the more I inevitably burden the prose with so much verbiage that it sinks of its own weight. Words get in the way of images. The big trick is deciding what *not* to say.

There's a sort of magic that transpires between writer and reader, an alchemy that occurs when two imaginations meet. If I write a book and a thousand people read it, I've really written a thousand books. Each reader brings his or her highly individual consciousness to the experience. Our imaginations are the product of everything we've done, been, said, and read; all the people we've known; and all the places we've been. The sum makes up our uniqueness. So each reader will approach a story differently and take something different away from it.

I constantly remind myself that I don't have to do all the work, and the more I do, the more I'm likely to get in the way. All I need is a few well-chosen words. If I write "cowboy," you'll supply your own image, based on your own experience. It probably won't be the cowboy I see in my own mind. But that's fine. Your cowboy is just as good as mine, probably better. My job as the writer is to give the magic, the alchemy, a chance to work.

Another big trick has to do with geometry.

I've never been much of a mathematician, but I've always liked geometry. And I finally figured out why: it's not about numbers, it's about logic. And that's what writing is about. Just as geometry organizes lines and angles into shapes, so writing logically organizes words into ideas.

A character has a shape, composed of those odd lines and angles that make up the thing we call humanity — each character, like each of us, unique and special. And my job as the writer is to portray that character, odd lines and angles and all, in a way that helps the reader to believe in him or her. I will find something of myself in each character. Perhaps you as reader will, too.

Stories also have a shape, a geometry. Characters bump up against each other and make sparks and set off actions and reactions. And the story assumes lines and angles that hopefully take logical form. As one writer friend puts it, "Stuff's gotta happen." And if what happens is something logical, the reader is more likely to take a leap of faith and become fully engaged with the story.

The trick is not to hurry, to allow the characters to shape the story; not to push or pull or manipulate but to let the tale take its natural course. The writer has to counsel himself to be patient, to give the characters room and time to reveal themselves. You no doubt have some idea of the broad shape of the story, of some major twists and turns that the tale will take, and how they might impact the characters. But the characters need room to move about within that framework, and to move things about if it suits them.

I had a chance to visit with Barry Hannah and to tell him how much his wisdom has meant to me over the years as I've struggled to become a decent writer. I've learned a couple of those big tricks he talked about. It's good to remember them in the throes of my ongoing agony.

How Much Do We Need to Know?

The late TV weatherman Clyde McLean used to tell this story:

"What's weather?" a youngster asked his father.

"Ask your mother," the father replied.

"But I don't want to know that much about weather," the youngster shot back.

In an age in which we are bombarded by information, it's an instructive story. How much do we really need to know? Is it possible to know too much?

My wife Paulette and I frequently watch the Weather Channel. We know the difference between a warm front and a cold front, although we are still a bit vague about occluded fronts. We are fairly knowledgeable about isobars, and we know that when they are packed tightly together on the weather map, it means windy conditions. We nod sagely when the Weather Channel folks show the jet stream, and we become ecstatic over entrenched high pressure systems.

But to what end? Do we know too much about the weather? Are we victims of weather overload?

Of course, there are lots of folks whose live-

lihoods depend on detailed weather forecasts —
farmers, fruit growers, paving contractors and the
like. Neither parents nor educators want school
buses on icy or snowy roads. And football fans
want to know whether to take umbrellas or sun
visors to the game.

Demand has driven supply. Weather fore-
casting has taken great strides, thanks to satellite
imagery and computer models. When your local
TV weathercaster says it's gonna rain buckets,
you'd probably better drag your galoshes out of
the closet.

But for most mere mortals, does the func-
tioning of our daily lives depend on intricate and
far-reaching knowledge of the weather? Probably
not. On most days, we may be like that small boy
in Clyde McLean's story. It might be refreshing to
occasionally take life and nature as it comes.

We might even sometimes assume the wary
attitude of the old farmer who entered the feed
and seed store and pronounced, "I heer'd on the
radio hit's a'gonna rain."

"That so?" another fellow said.

"Yep, said the farmer, "but I don't know
whether to believe it or not. I heer'd it on one of
them little cheap sets."

This business of knowledge also applies to
measuring things. We have a modern passion for
exactitude. We judge computers by megabytes of
RAM and gigabytes of drive space. We know to
the inch how far it is to the moon or the top of
Mount Mitchell. We know the precise size of the
federal debt and the exact destructive power of
weapons. Do we sometimes wish we didn't?

I started thinking about this when a fellow
delivered a load of firewood to my home. He assured me that the wood was of sufficient age to

burn well. He didn't give me a scientific measurement of the moisture content, he simply said, "Mister Bob, that wood is dry as dust." How beautifully descriptive. An exaggeration, of course, but the wood does exactly what it's intended to do. It burns, and burns well. That's all I needed to know.

When I was growing up, there were two brothers in my hometown who were carpenters. Otha was a precise fellow, never more comfortable than when equipped with tape measure, T-square and plumb. Anse took a more general approach. He could stick his arm out and sight over an upraised thumb and build you a wall as true and square as any Otha could measure. Anse would grumble, "We could get a whole lot more work done if Otha wouldn't do so dang much measuring." Each had his technique. Both worked. But Anse outlived Otha by several years. It wasn't the measuring, it was the *attitude* about measuring, I believe, that served him well.

Now, Lord knows, I'm not arguing for ignorance. I believe passionately that knowledge makes us free and contributes to the general improvement of humankind. Knowledge is the bulwark of an energetic and democratic society. The suppression of knowledge is the work of charlatans and despots.

Perhaps the issue is not knowledge, but rather information. There's a difference. We need to know, in the broadest sense of the word, but we need to be selective about the information we absorb. It's like making coffee without putting a filter in the pot. We get a lot of grounds.

Too much random information can numb our spirits and crowd out the kinds of things that can't be measured: love, compassion, faith, reason. If our brains are in overdrive, our souls may lie fallow. We need more time to feel, to listen to our hearts.

I think I'll start by taking a week off from the Weather Channel. I'll miss the jet stream. But I may sleep better.

A Guide to Political Approximation

In my first job in TV news years ago, I had the delightful experience of working with a colleague named George Mitchell. He was a charming and good-hearted fellow, but perhaps his most endearing trait was that he was not hung up on nomenclature.

George's two favorite words were "doojigger" and "doomaflotchie." The spelling here is approximate, as was George's use of the terms. If he couldn't think of the name of something, he called it either a doomaflotchie or a doojigger. On any given day, a doojigger might refer to a wide-angle lens, a roll of film, a Snickers bar, or gas for the news vehicle; a doomaflotchie might be a camera, a pencil, or directions to the scene of whatever story we were covering. All of the above, including the Snickers bar, are essential to a crack team of reporters.

As we would sprint out the back door of the newsroom, enroute to cover another exciting meeting of the Rotary Club, George would yell, "Did you get the doojigger?" The first few times this happened, I would stop dead in my tracks and stare at him. "The what?" "Oh, you know that, ah, doomaflotchie thing." If we had time, I would make George physically show me the object he was talking about. If we didn't, we would speed off to the news scene. And invariably, when we got there, we would find that we had forgotten the doojigger or the doomaflotchie. We made do.

I realized after working with George for awhile that the precise naming of things was simply not something he considered a priority. He was an excellent reporter, a stickler for facts about an event or personage. But when it came to equipment, he was, well, approximate. It could be maddening. I never knew from one day to the next what a doojigger or doomaflotchie might be. But George was a happy man, at peace with himself and the world. I learned to admire his approach to life.

I think about George Mitchell every time we are on the verge of another election. It occurs to me that candidates for political office are prone to the same sort of approximations as my friend George. They orate in generalities and thrive on imprecision. When we hear one of them speak, we are inclined to wonder, "What did he say?" This doesn't seem to bother the candidates, and the rest of us have become pretty well resigned to it.

Many candidates may do this without realizing what they are doing. But it's more effective, I think, if it's deliberate. With that in mind, here are a few nuggets of advice for candidates about approximation:

1. When running for office, either take an outrageous position or none at all. The cleverest tack is the latter. One of my favorite North Caro-

lina politicians of some years ago was the late W.T. Harris, who served with distinction on the Mecklenburg county commission. During one election, I asked him for his position on a controversial issue. "Oh," said Mr. Harris, "I'm all right on that one." He kept getting elected and eventually had a boulevard named for him. So there.

2. Invent issues with which you can befuddle the electorate and confound the opposition. In one southern U.S. Senate race some years ago, a fellow who had made his name in statewide politics was pitted against a member of the U.S. Congress. The state politician accused his opponent of being part of the "Washington crowd." He never explained what that meant, or why it was so terrible, but the way he said "Washington crowd" made it sound akin to "child molester." The state politician won handily and promptly became part of the "Washington crowd."

3. Claim poverty of campaign resources, whether it's true or not. If you win, you can say that you have overcome great odds and will be seen as a champion of the common folk. If you lose, you can always say you were outspent.

4. Either take credit or assess blame, depending on which does you the most good. If you are an incumbent, give yourself credit for every good thing that has happened during your tenure in office, including the fact that no ships have been sunk by icebergs on inland rivers in your jurisdiction. If you are a challenger, blame the incumbent with every ill, including volcanic eruptions on Monserrat.

5. Above all, be imprecise and approximate. If you don't want to deal with something, call it a doojigger. If you want to tar your opponent with a label that will make him hang his head in shame,

call him a doomaflotchie.

In any campaign, the candidates seem to do much of the above without much prompting. But it never hurts to remind. If the campaign proceeds according to precedent, we'll be rewarded by government of doojigger and doomaflotchie.

George Mitchell would be proud.

The Best $200 Million Hollywood Ever Spent

When the movie *Titanic* was enjoying its first run in the theatres, I only saw it once. And I haven't revisited it since then, even though it's on the shelf at every video rental store and even occasionally on cable TV. The reason is, I was so profoundly moved by the experience, I'm still savoring my original, pristine impression. Later, maybe, I'll watch it to dissect the art and craft of filmmaking that made such an impact on me and millions of others. But not yet.

But I seem to be an exception. When the movie was in theatres worldwide, audiences were full of people who had seen *Titanic* three, four, seven times.

Why were we so taken with this film? Is it the $200 million budget? The attractive young stars? The love story? The epic nature of the tragic historical event that underpins the plot? The special effects? The sheer size of it? The audacity of director James Cameron?

Yes to all, and to any other reason you can come up with. It's the total package, and for that — for putting it all together into a memorable experience — we can thank Cameron. The man could *see* the whole movie in his head, and he had the vision, the arrogance, the chutzpah to make it happen. When studio bean counters complained about the spiraling costs, he fought them and won. He took no guff from the actors. He drove them and the crew mercilessly, to performances they probably didn't know they had in them. And the result, in my mind, is a monumental achievement in filmmaking.

So I toast James Cameron, and that's hard to do for a writer of movies. I've written several, and like many of my fellow writers, I regard directors with both admiration and suspicion.

Some years ago, a great director came up with the *auteur* theory — which says, in short, that the director is the "author" of a movie. The notion raises the hackles of writers who protest, "If you don't have a script, you don't have a movie." That's true. But I've come to learn through years in the business that a script is not a movie, only a blueprint for one.

Filmmaking is a process of collaborative creation. It begins with a writer who spins out a yarn on paper — characters, plot, dialogue, stage direction — all meeting the special demands of film.

A book tells much of its story by illuminating the minds of the characters. Author and reader know what characters think as well as what they do and say. But film can see only obliquely into a character's mind and soul. Everything internal has to be externalized with scene-setting, action, and dialogue. The flip side is that the screenwriter doesn't have to tell us what scenes and characters look like. We can see and hear for ourselves.

Eventually, the writer must turn loose of the material. And that's where the director takes over. It's his or her job to turn a nightmare of detail into a finished film — a general leading a small army, often against great odds. The director shepherds the talents of many — writer, cast, crew, support troops — and has the force and vision to lead them to the conclusion of battle. Whether it's a victory or not, the customers decide.

In the process of turning script into film, the writer may get lost in the shuffle. Writers complain that directors often change their scripts with impunity and make unrecognizable muddles of the finished product. Many writers consider themselves second-class citizens in the film world, treated by directors with condescension, disdain, even outright hostility.

That has not been my experience. I've mostly worked with directors who respect my effort and involve me throughout the process. In turn, I recognize and respect their indispensable role in making my scripts come alive. I am the author of the script, but the director is the author of the film. It's not my movie, it's ours.

Some writers aspire to direct their own scripts so they can retain "creative control." James Cameron is among them. For *Titanic,* he is both writer and director, and splendid as both.

My impression, from seeing the movie just once, is that it is a fine script. Some critics have called the dialogue "cheesy," and perhaps it is to the modern ear. But it accurately reflects the innocence of both the characters and the age in which the story takes place. As interpreted by talented actors, it moves the characters through an arc of life-changing experience that audiences obviously found honest and fulfilling.

I'm partial to movies that are about characters (*The English Patient* and *Amistad* are two of my recent favorites). In some ways, James Cameron's achievement in *Titanic* goes beyond that — making a cataclysmic event both human and cataclysmic, and making both elements work as a seamless whole. I've never seen anything quite like it. Someday I'll see it again.

Next at 11: More Mayhem and Misery

I was in Los Angeles when I read the newspaper headline: VIOLENT CRIME DOWN 12.4%.

"Oh, boy!" I said to myself. "Now the local TV news shows will cut their coverage of crime by 12.4%." So I tuned in to the 11:00 Los Angeles news.

The lead story was about a high-speed chase. When police tried to arrest a man for a traffic violation, he sped off in his pickup truck. The chase ended when the man smashed his truck into an automobile. The auto caught fire. Officers managed to get the woman driver out just before it blew up. Then they arrested the pickup driver. Ambulances carted away the pickup driver and the woman in the car.

It was a television news dream story. It had a crime, a culprit, a victim, a high-speed chase, a wreck, roaring flames, police with guns. Every TV station in Los Angeles had a crew on the scene to capture the high drama on videotape. Every 11:00 newscast in town had the pictures. And more than eighteen hours later, the stations were still showing the same pictures. There really wasn't much new information, but the pictures were just too good to give up.

Over the three days I was in Los Angeles, I watched several local TV newscasts. And if they had reduced their crime coverage by even one percent, I couldn't tell it. The news was a steady diet of shootings, wrecks, fires, weird goings-on and anti-social behavior. And when they ran out of such stories in California, they searched far afield. One local Los Angeles newscast had a story about a hoax telephone call in South Carolina.

Now, maybe I'm judging Los Angeles TV news too harshly. Maybe violent crime in that area *isn't* down. Maybe there just wasn't anything going on in the schools, local government, the economy or cultural activities that week. But the Los Angeles newscasts look suspiciously like those in virtually every city I've visited in the past few years. TV news, like the Vietnam War, is becoming obsessed with body count. And as the body count goes up, viewership goes down.

Why is local TV news so consumed with mayhem and misery? I can think of at least a couple of reasons.

The first is fairly obvious: the entertainment factor. A newspaper is primarily an informational medium. But television is mostly entertainment. TV news used to be an island of information in the midst of that entertainment sea. But over the years, the lines have gotten increasingly blurred. It's all driven by video. As one local TV news director told me some years ago, "If it don't wiggle, it ain't television." And the more wiggle, the better. Flames, body bags and smashed metal are more interesting to look at than elected officials sitting around a table deciding things like where our kids go to school.

The second reason is less obvious: economics. Wrecks, fires and crimes are cheap to cover. It may take a reporter and a photographer all day, or even several days, to put together a good TV news story about education or employment. But when somebody gets shot, the newsroom can send a photographer to the scene to roll off a little videotape and jot down the name of an investigating officer who can be called later for details. Even if a reporter goes along to interview the officer and witnesses, it's a brief business.

As competition from cable and satellite has grown, broadcast TV stations have pared expenses to preserve profits. In a labor-intensive business, that means cutting people. News departments are required to air more hours of news with smaller staffs. So they fill up those hours with stories that are quick, easy and cheap to cover. Mayhem and misery — much of it, not even local. And those stories crowd out the news we really need to know — news about our work, our families, our schools, our churches, our health and pocketbooks.

It's a self-defeating strategy. Television has to compete for viewers' attention with all those other demands on our time. And a busy viewer who tunes in to a newscast and finds it largely irrelevant to his or her daily life isn't likely to consider news viewing a priority.

One friend in TV news says the industry is driven by fear — fear of intense competition, of shrinking audience, of diminished profit. If that's so, the industry might want to consider airing a product that we consumers of news find useful and necessary.

Human nature being what it is, TV stations aren't likely to run out of bodies. But they may well run out of viewers, and sooner than they think.

End of School Advice: Hug a Teacher

Whenever the end of a school year rolls around, I always have a bit of advice for young folks, especially for graduating seniors. Seek out your favorite teacher and tell him or her how much he or she has meant to you. I guarantee that it will do wonders for the spirits of an overworked, underpaid person who is, at that point in the year, nearing the end of patience, stamina and good humor.

Not long ago, I got to give my favorite teacher a hug and to tell her — as I've done often through the years — the profound impact she has had on my life. It made me feel good to do so. I think it made her feel pretty special, too.

Miriam Kennedy was a member of the church I attended as a boy, but I didn't really know her very well until I encountered her in the seventh grade. She was a tiny woman, almost fragile looking. Seventh grade boys, even those of the tamer 1950's, are by nature prone to test limits of authority. Each class that came along tested Mrs. Kennedy only once, was promptly routed from the field of battle, and beat a hasty retreat into cowed obedience. "Dynamite," Mrs. Kennedy liked to say, "comes in small packages."

So we quickly found out who was boss and settled in to learn English the Miriam Kennedy way. It was meat and potatoes stuff. We first learned the parts of speech — their names, their definitions, their practical usage. *A noun is the name of a person, place, thing or idea.* It was a sort of catechism that we memorized and repeated over and over — aloud in class and in our sleep at night — until nouns, verbs, adjectives, adverbs and the like became second nature. That mastered, we moved on to the rules of grammar and punctuation.

Once Mrs. Kennedy was satisfied that we had the basics down pat, she taught us how to use all those parts of speech as the building blocks of sentences. We did it by making diagrams of the sentences, putting each word in its proper place and seeing graphically how it fit with every other word. We started with simple declarative sentences and moved on to compound and complex stuff. By the end of the year, we could take just about any horribly tricky jumble of words that Mrs. Kennedy could throw at us and make a thing of geometric beauty out of it.

Mrs. Kennedy was also our English teacher the next year in eighth grade. So by the time she turned us loose into the rarified atmosphere of high school, we were proficient with language. We could speak it properly, and use it on paper in a way that others could easily understand. And we were ready to take on "literature," to see the words that others had written in a new light and appreciate the form and substance of their thoughts.

I've often thought of written language as the

logical expression of an organized mind. Miriam Kennedy, by teaching us language from the ground up, helped to organize our chaotic little junior high minds. She taught us, more than language alone, *ways of thinking.* And what we learned from her in that respect, we applied in every other subject — math, science, social studies, foreign language. We still do.

There is a facet to the process of writing that is much like architecture — words fitting together the way the elements of a building do. It's like building a house: a foundation, a framework, walls and roof, then the interior. It's the place where your characters live. Fashioning a complex tale out of individual words and sentences. Logic and organization, married to imagination. The craft of writing, married to the art.

When I gave Mrs. Kennedy a hug not long ago, I told her again that when I go to my keyboard each morning to work on whatever piece of writing occupies me at the moment, she is always at my elbow. What I know of grammar, punctuation, parts of speech and sentence structure, I learned from her. The lessons are just as clear today as when she drummed them into me and my classmates in the seventh and eighth grades. Whatever success I have had as a writer, I owe a great deal of the credit to Miriam Kennedy.

There's an extra dividend to all this. Mrs. Kennedy was ever the strict disciplinarian, but it became abundantly clear to all her students that she cared deeply about us, that she expected the best from us, and that she was, above all, our friend. She still is.

Somewhere in every student's life there's a Mrs. Kennedy. Before the final bell, give her a hug. She deserves a lot more, but a hug will do for starters.

On a Journey to a Far Country

I'm setting out on a journey to a far country. If you don't hear from me on a regular basis, send out a posse.

I'm not going on a trip, not in physical terms, I'm starting a new book. It is, in every sense of the word, a visit to another place. I've done this before, and I know a little about the kind of landscape I'll be traversing. For some of the time, I'll be thrashing about in underbrush, trying to find the path. If experience is any teacher, I'll eventually find it, not through any unerring sense of direction on my part, but because of the help of friends.

The best fiction, I believe, is driven by its characters. As we read, we watch mere mortals struggle through all manner of dilemmas, many of them challenges of the soul. We find bits and pieces of ourselves in those characters and, by living with them through the pages of the story, gain insight into our own peculiar struggles. That's what happens with reading. That's also what happens with writing.

Over the course of my story in the months ahead, I'll meet its characters and they will become my friends. I've started, as I always do, with one particular person in a particular time and place — a person afflicted with a personal crisis that I find intriguing. As the story marches on, this main character begets others. Some have already occurred to me. Many others, I haven't the foggiest notion about at this point. They'll simply appear and join the cast. Some, I'll like. Others, I won't. Some will make me leap with joy. Others will aggravate me no end. Most will be a curious mixture of saint and sinner. As are we all.

So, I start with characters, this motley assortment of folk who will lead me out of the underbrush. I try mightily to be honest with them — to present them as they are, warts and all, to let them make a story through their human commerce with each other. If I try to manipulate them, try to shove them in a direction they don't want to go or imbue them with characteristics they don't honestly have, they'll tell me to back off. My job as chronicler of their story is to follow along at a respectful distance and write down what they do and say. I know that sounds a little mystical, but for me, that's the way it works.

I admit to being the sloppiest of storytellers when it comes to organizing a novel. I don't outline, at least not in any detail, and not at all on paper. My mind is like a storage closet, crammed over the years with assorted junk — bits and pieces of history, old fruitcakes (some of them human), tennis racquets and shotguns. When I write a story, I open the closet and stuff tumbles out. I pick up what I can use at the moment and cram the rest back inside the closet to be revisited later. I throw out nothing. Eventually, much of what I've saved becomes useful, often in a most surprising way.

I don't particularly recommend this approach to writing something as complicated as a novel. During the process, I'm beset with trepidations and night sweats. "There's got to be an easier way!" I cry. If there is, I'm not capable of it. For better or worse, I'm condemned to be a footsore pilgrim, stumbling along the path behind my characters, ultimately trusting them to lead us through. What will happen along the way? I know a few major things going in, but I have to be open to possibility, which is the essence of human experience. Much will reveal itself.

So, I start with character. And then there's discipline, the stubborn insistence on continuing the journey day after day.

My favorite writer story is about Sinclair Lewis, who was invited to speak on his art and craft at an Ivy League college years ago. Mr. Lewis was inclined to take a nip, and this particular evening he had taken several. When he was introduced, he stumbled onstage and peered bleary-eyed at his audience of several hundred students. "How many of you wanna write?" he asked. Every hand in the place went up. "Then why the hell aren't you home writing?" he bellowed, and staggered off the stage. That was it.

Some writers have to be dragged kicking and screaming. Others spring from bed in outrageous good spirit every morning and dash to the worktable. I fall somewhere in between. On many days, I'm enthusiastically inspired. On others, I simply don't feel like writing. But I find that if I go forth faithfully each day and patiently wait for my characters to speak and act, I write about as well on those days I don't feel like doing it, as on those I do.

Years ago, when I finished graduate school, I announced grandly to my good wife, "I want to write a novel."

"Fine," she said. "Get a real job and write in your spare time. I want the girls to have dancing lessons." For years, I wrote in my spare time.

Three novels, some movie scripts, a good bit of other stuff. Now, the girls are grown (both graceful from the dance) and writing *is* my real job. It waits to be done. As I say, a journey to a far country.

The Life We Might Lead

Mel Torme was one of my favorite singers, and his voice was one of the most distinctive to grace American popular music in this century. The first time I saw him was on a television variety show back in the 50's — Milton Berle, I think it was. Berle called him "the kid with the gauze in his jaws." He did, indeed, have a sort of gauzy, opaque voice, a little like smooth whiskey being strained through silk. He was better known in musical circles as "The Velvet Fog," which was even more descriptive. When Mel Torme died last year, I learned that he disliked the name and what it stood for.

Torme started performing on the radio at age four, and by the time he finished high school in 1943, he had decided he wanted to be a jazz singer. But his manager thought he'd do better as what was known in those days as a "crooner," a singer of popular ballads. Torme described his early efforts as "mushy, sentimental songs," the sort that led to the Velvet Fog description. He realized that he had gotten sidetracked, going for commercial success instead of the kind of music that was his heart and soul. He spent the rest of his life becoming the jazz singer he originally intended to be. He described his vocal career as a work in progress, "a long learning curve."

How wonderful, I thought when I read Mel Torme's obituary. Here was a young man enjoying early, and no doubt heady success as a crooner. Hit records, money rolling in, fans clamoring to see and hear him, critics saying nice things in the paper. And yet, it wasn't what he intended. So he spent more than forty years reinventing himself. And when he died at age seventy-three, he was indeed a jazz singer. One of the very best. Had he lived another thirty years, I suspect he would have still been reinventing himself.

Mel Torme would have liked Carl Sandburg, who spent his entire lifetime not "being," but "becoming." Sandburg is best known, I suppose, as a poet. But during his long and productive life he was, at times, a traveling folksinger, a hobo, a furnace stoker, a journalist, a biographer, and a historian. By the time he moved to the North Carolina mountains near Flat Rock to write and live out his days, he had bitten off a big chunk of life. As you tour the rooms of his Flat Rock home and see the awesome variety of books he collected, you get a sense of how much he did and how much interested him. Sandburg never stopped reading, thinking, questioning, wondering — and reinventing himself.

Sandburg's writing celebrates the great diversity of his life, and here again he was always trying something new. He wrote a six-volume biography of Abraham Lincoln, a monumental work of research and literary craftsmanship. You'd think he might finish something like that and rest on his laurels, his reputation secure. But no, he went on to new endeavors, always challenging himself, always expanding the limits of his abilities. He was a sort of intellectual vagabond — an explorer and entrepreneur — whose mind and interests wandered across the vast landscape of human possibility.

Sometimes, people like Mel Torme and Carl Sandburg lend their vision to business enterprises. Two of the American companies I admire the most are Hewlett-Packard and Intel, and the reason I respect them so much is because they're not afraid to reinvent themselves, even at times when you might think they should stand pat and play it safe.

Hewlett-Packard is one of our legendary business stories. It was started in a garage in Palo Alto, California by two engineers who wanted to build scientific measurement instruments. H-P still manufactures some of those, but the present-day list of the company's products is mind-boggling. We consumers probably know H-P best for its computers and printers, but it has a finger in just about every high-tech pie imaginable. Between that modest beginning and today's industrial-technical giant, the people who ran H-P kept looking for new things to develop and manufacture, even when the new product might make a present, successful one obsolete.

The same is true at Intel, the world's foremost inventor and manufacturer of computer chips. What Intel makes today is highly profitable. But you can bet that back in the lab, scientists are developing chips and other products that we can scarcely imagine, products that will make today's inventory obsolete, even while it might still have a useful life. They're taking risks. Staying ahead of the curve. Reinventing the company.

I think there's a lesson in this for all of us.

If we stand pat, play things safe, hole up in our smug, self-satisfied worlds, we stagnate. We need to challenge ourselves, take some risks, be open to possibility, reinvent. Like Torme and Sandburg, Hewlett-Packard and Intel.

A character in one of my novels says that we each have two lives: the one we actually live, and the one we *might* live. It's intriguing to consider what we might be, the way we might reinvent ourselves. The one thing for sure about that other life — we won't find it unless we go looking for it.